Real Men Do It Outdoors

Real Men Do It Outdoors
The Blokes'
BBQ Cookbook

Joshua Barnes

LONGUEVILLE
BOOKS

CONTENTS

Introduction   8
Where there's smoke, there's fire – a guide to BBQ safety   10
Anatomy of a BBQ – a guide to all those unknown parts   10
Instructions – who needs them anyway?   12
Don't get burnt – get what you paid for   13
Now you're cooking with gas – the BBQ evolution   14
Covered cooking down under   16
Scrubbers guide to minimal cleaning and maintenance   18

THE RECIPES   20–116

FEATURES

Size matters   48
Cow cuts   66
Sheep cuts   68
Bangers for sangers   70
Veggies mate!   72
Herbs and spices   74
Accessories   78
Spices, rubs and bastes   86
Reasons why it's ok to spend your kids' college fund on a new BBQ   90
Barbecue etiquette   92
Preparing for the big day   94
Cure for the common … hangover   106
Bush BBQs   116
Best beers for the day   118
Backyard cricket rules   122
Index to recipes   124

INTRODUCTION

IF IT SEEMS LIKE THIS BOOK WAS
written by a bloke sitting in his backyard
at an unstable outdoor setting, gazing at
his BBQ while typing very slowly with one
finger and clutching a beer in the other
hand you'd be right. It was tough work but
hey, someone had to do it!

Why write a book about backyard
wbarbecuing? Well it's simple; I love
everything about it, from sunny Aussie
weekends to backyard cricket, tall tales
marinaded in dry humour and most
importantly a brilliant excuse to fob off all
weekend chores in order to down cold
stubbies while charcoaling huge chunks of
meat under the Australian sun.

What we have in this book are REAL
recipes that WORK. They will impress
your mates and keep the girls happy
because you're giving them time to chat
with ▮▮▮▮▮ds. In Real Men do it
Out▮▮▮▮▮l find:

- the perfect steak sandwich
- how to bake the big one that didn't
  get away
- pizza on the BBQ
- the ultimate rissole recipe, and
- we throw some shrimps – let's call them
  prawns here – on the barbie.

But BBQs aren't just about food. They
are an excuse to spend as much time
as possible with close friends doing as
little as possible. Time creatively filled
with pointless debates about topics that
have no real answers, yarns about events
that never really happened and most
importantly quality time set aside to have a
laugh with your best mates.

Real Men Do It Outdoors will provide
you with all the essentials required to
enjoy endless Aussie BBQs, starting with
reasons why it's ok to spend your kids'
College fund on a new BBQ and, after
much debate, why barbecuing is better
than sex.

Only then will you really understand
why real men do it outdoors!

WHERE THERE'S SMOKE, THERE'S FIRE A GUIDE TO BBQ SAFETY

REAL MEN DO IT OUTDOORS TAKES A light-hearted look at backyard barbecuing in Australia and does not replace the official manufacturer's rules, regulations and guidelines for BBQ use and safety.

It is important you always refer to the instruction manuals, warranties and safety guides provided by the manufacturer as these are written with particular BBQs in mind and may vary between manufacturers.

It's really recommended you read this section before cracking open a case and settling in for the afternoon.

These safety tips are designed to help you avoid blowing yourself up. So, put down the beer – I know you have one – and pay attention.

■ Most important – always fully read the safety instructions. Each new BBQ should include a set of instructions outlining important procedures to ensure safe preparation and ongoing use of your BBQ. If these are not included, contact the manufacturer or the place of purchase.

■ Most obvious – gas is flammable! It may seem strange to many of you that I'm pointing this out. But in the excitement that accompanies a new BBQ, many people forget the danger. Remember, the longer you leave the gas running before lighting, the bigger the flame. If the BBQ doesn't light first go, turn it off and wait at least 30 seconds for the unused gas to clear before trying again.

■ Indoor use – Ensure all fittings are securely tightened, gas burners are correctly sitting over the gas cocks and there are no gas leaks. To check this prior to use, run soapy water over all connections; if you see bubbles re-tighten and test again.

■ Regularly check the hose and regulator for cracks and leaks. If in doubt, throw them out.

■ Cylinders – these are to be treated like your schooner glasses. Always ensure they remain upright and out of direct sunlight. When the cylinder gets too old get it checked or get a new one – approximately every 10 years. There should be a stamp on the side of the bottle indicating the date when the bottle was last tested, but if in doubt contact your gas supplier for advice.

■ Fat/oil – always keep the drip tray full of a fat-absorbing substance to prevent fat fires occurring. You may find this type of fire is not covered by warranties, so don't cut corners.

n Indoor use – BBQs are not designed to be used indoors. If it rains, build a pergola, or order a pizza.

■ If you don't know exactly what you are doing, especially with regulators, hoses, and gas lines, don't try to be a 'mister fix it'. Use official parts and consult professionals; $10 for a new part is cheaper than the burns unit!

No more lectures. Sit back, relax, crack a coldie and get on with the barbie.

ANATOMY OF A BBQ – A GUIDE TO ALL THOSE UNKNOWN PARTS

1. Frame – steel frame covered in paint or vitreous enamel.
2. Trolley – holds BBQ up; often metal and/or timber.
3. Roasting Hood – turns BBQ into roasting oven.
4. Rain Lid – protects cooking surface from the weather; not for roasting.
5. Hose & Regulator – left hand thread; regulates gas flow; connects BBQ to cylinder.
6. Gas Cylinder/Bottle – fuel source; turn off between use (turn burners off first).
7. Plates and Grills – generally cast iron or steel; always keep well oiled.
8. Burners – source of heat. Cast iron or metal; sit over gas cocks.

9. Drip Tray – catches fat from food; always fill with recommended fat-absorbing material to prevent fat fires.
10. Rock Tray – distributes heat evenly under grill; requires lava/ceramic rock.
11. Flame Tamers/Diverters – distributes heat evenly under grill; does not require lava/ceramic rock.
12. Lava/Ceramic Rock – sits on top of rock tray, replace regularly.
13. Auto Ignition – built-in ignition system for your BBQ.
14. Gas Cocks – feeds gas from manifold to burners.
15. Side Burner – for wok cooking.
16. Manifold – supplies gas to burners.

INSTRUCTIONS – WHO NEEDS THEM ANYWAY?

In life men hold certain rights and responsibilities. These include knowledge of all things metal and fuel driven, the ability to read road maps and most importantly the right to ignore all instruction manuals. Failure to live up to these rules may result in the downfall of all mankind.

The main reason instructions are so difficult to read in the first place is because the person who wrote them, did so without referring to the 'How to formulate clear and simple instruction booklets' booklet.

It also serves as a reminder to all those weak individuals who refer to instructions before starting a task that it would have been quicker and easier to have skipped the instructions in the first place. Even then, you should try and try again before giving up.

So as an alternative we have provided a cheater's guide to BBQ assembly.

This is never to be confused with instruction booklets, often recognised by numbered incoherent rules, which make no sense, and go around in circles to cause confusion, with numbers and rules incoherent, making circles and causing sense with booklets.

5-STEP CHEATER'S GUIDE TO BUILDING YOUR BBQ

1. Open the box and tip everything onto the ground
2. Build the trolley by firstly assembling upside down
3. Bolt BBQ to the frame (still upside down)
4. Stand up and further tighten all bolts, then add burners plates and grills
5. Test for gas leaks and cure plates before cooking

DON'T GET BURNT – GET WHAT YOU PAID FOR

ALTHOUGH ALL BBQS APPEAR SIMILAR on the surface there are a number of differences to keep an eye out for to ensure you are getting the best quality BBQ your money can afford.

The following are questions you should ask to ensure you are getting exactly what you paid for:

WHAT EXACTLY DO I GET FOR THE PRICE?

You don't want to be left with a number of additional costs that blow your budget, so use this first BBQ buyer's check list:

USUALLY INCLUDED AS STANDARD

BBQ frame
Trolley
Rain lid
Burners
Flame tamer/diverter or rock tray
Cooking plates and grills
Hose and regulator
Drip tray
Auto ignition system

AVAILABLE SEPARATELY OR AS PART OF A PACKAGE

Gas cylinder
Gas
Roasting hood
Fat absorbing product for drip tray

WHAT IS THE FINISH ON THE FRAME AND ROASTING HOOD?

The finish of the BBQ will impact greatly on the overall price and quality of the BBQ. Be sure to ask whether both the frame and the roasting hood are coated in the same quality finish.

Powder coated or baked enamel – this coating will be found on most low-mid level BBQs. The paint can be scratched or burnt off if the heat is too high, eventually resulting in rust.

Vitreous enamel – this is a much higher quality finish due to the glass/enamel coating which is fused on at much higher temperatures. It is a longer-lasting scratch- and heat-resistant finish.

Stainless steel – an ideal finish if you live in areas near the ocean as it is rust-resistant against the salty sea breeze. The weight of steel used in the frame can vary dramatically and will affect the strength and quality of the BBQ.

DOES THE COST INCLUDE ASSEMBLY AND DELIVERY OF THE BBQ?

This will vary depending upon the value of the BBQ, store policy and your negotiation skills. Many powder-coated or lower end BBQs do not include this service.

DOES THE RETAILER HOLD SPARE PARTS AND PROVIDE STRONG AFTER SALES SERVICE?

There is nothing worse than getting home to find that a component is missing or broken and having to wait a week while the part is ordered especially when you have organised a party the next day.

DO ALL BBQS REQUIRE A HOSE AND REGULATOR?

All BBQs should be supplied with their own hose and regulator except for some small camping BBQs which control gas flow via a high pressure hose. Always refer to manufacturer guidelines.

IF YOU HAVE ACCESS TO NATURAL GAS DOES THE BBQ COME WITH A CONVERSION KIT?

You should be able to run your BBQ from natural gas. To do this you will need to change the gas jets to suit natural gas, which should be available from most BBQ retailers.

WHAT PLATE AND GRILL ARRANGEMENTS ARE AVAILABLE?

Most new BBQs come with half plate and half grill as standard. If you prefer more plate or more grill try to negotiate this as part of your deal.

Most manufacturers recommend you include part grill to allow some heat to escape, help the upward draft under the plate and grills and to help prevent the flame from being forced down into the drip tray which can start fat fires.

DO SIDE BURNERS FIT ONTO ALL BBQS?

This will vary depending upon type of BBQ trolley you have. It's often easiest to get one included up front, plus this will encourage you to experiment and spend more time cooking outdoors.

NOW YOU'RE COOKING WITH GAS – THE BBQ EVOLUTION

THERE IS A CERTAIN allure to creating your own BBQ from freshly chopped wood, discarded branches, bark or charcoal plus whatever you think will burn, you can find around the camping ground.
However, it's not very often these days that you get the big thumbs up to pile up a heap of flammable crap and set it alight.

Although it's becoming increasingly difficult to use campfires – with the low water levels and high fire dangers across summer – one thing we can be sure of is, there will always be a divide between the smoke and flames from a pile of raw timber' advocates and the new age 'gas is quicker and cleaner' advocates.

I agree charcoal BBQs create a unique flavour and every now and then are well worth the effort. However, if you're like me and BBQ every chance you get, the thought of lighting charcoal with kero-scented firelighters, drowning your backyard in smoke and waiting extended periods is far from ideal.
You also need to balance

uneven heat and then remove ash from the food before extinguishing the fire if it hasn' already burnt out.

Alternatively, you could quite easily sit back and watch the food simmer away on the clean instant heat provided by gas. Time better spent downing a couple of coldies while watching sport.

Personally I'm happy to sacrifice a small amount of flavour for the ease and simplicity of gas. The bottom line is, if you're barbequing and having a great time, who cares how you do it, as long as you do it outdoors!

COVERED COOKING
DOWN UNDER

THINKING BACK TO childhood, BBQs were straight-forward flat plates and grill set-ups, used primarily for cooking snags, steaks and onions.

These days the backyard BBQ is no longer equivalent to a benchtop stove but is more like an entire modern kitchen allowing you to grill, bake, deep-fry, and roast, with additional advantages such as fat-reduction cooking, easier cleaning and reduced heat in your home during summer.

The best kept secret is the brownie points you will receive from your lovely lady for spending hours outside ' slaving' over the hot BBQ. In this context 'slaving' is defined as clicking the auto ignition, throwing on the meat, putting your feet up, drinking beer, catching rays and talking crap with your mates, followed by under-a-minute cleaning.

Alternatively, you can be stuck in a boiling kitchen while your mates sit outside watching sport and wondering why you weren't in the important third slip position near the esky prior to drinks break of the ultimate backyard cricket challenge – kitchen cricket doesn't quite have the same ring to it.

For good reason covered cooking BBQ is becoming the norm.

TECHNIQUES FOR ROASTING

In principle, roasting in a BBQ is very similar to roasting in an oven, only with the benefits of added flavour and being outdoors.

If the food allows, we recommend you remove the solid plate from your BBQ, leaving only the grill, allowing better heat flow under the hood. With this done, push the grill into the centre, creating a platform on which you place your roast-holder or baking dish. If you don't have these items, simply place the food on the grill.

Start by lighting all four burners then close the hood and heat to the desired temperature. Most hoods will have a temperature gauge on the front; if not you can buy them at all good BBQ stores.

Once at the required temperature, turn the centre burners off so no direct heat is generated under the grill and reduce the burner flames on each side of the grill to a low–medium heat.

Add the roast holder, meat and drip pan before closing the hood.

Try not to open the hood to check the meat as this will cause the temperature to fluctuate and extend the cooking time.

Cook for the time outlined in the recipe using the two indirect burners to control the temperature. When you reach the time when it is due to be ready, use a meat thermometer to check the internal heat of the meat to confirm it's ready.

ADDITIONAL TIPS
To ensure a tender, juicy, roast you may also include a small container of water next to the roast to stop it drying out.

During the roasting process, it is important that you enjoy cold beers and backyard cricket.

SCRUBBERS GUIDE TO MINIMAL CLEANING AND MAINTENANCE

POSSIBLY THE GREATEST advantage of outdoor cooking over conventional kitchen cooking is the small amount of effort required to keep the BBQ clean.

The following is a guide only; always refer to your specific BBQ instructions to ensure you are treating your BBQ correctly.

COOKING SURFACE

The one golden rule for maintaining the perfect cooking surface is 'you can never use too much cooking oil when cleaning'. Once used, at no time should the cooking surface come in contact with soap or water.

After cooking, scrape off any excess food and grime and apply an extra coating of oil to the plate to protect it between uses.

After the BBQ has cooled down, remember to replace the rain lid to protect the cooking surface from the elements.

Before re-using, heat the BBQ and repeat the process.

BBQ FRAME AND ROASTING HOOD

If your BBQ looks as though it has reached the point of no return or you are looking for an effort-free alternative, you'll find barbie cleaning sprays at all major retailers. This is a little like oven cleaner for the barbie.

TROLLEYS

Hardwood trolleys should be treated regularly with natural oil to prevent the wood from drying, fading and cracking.

Due to hardwood expanding or contracting as the weather changes, the bolts holding the trolley together will occasionally need to be tightened.

Metal trolley scratches should be touched up with a standard metal paint to avoid rust.

DRIP TRAY

The drip tray will need to be cleaned out and refilled with a fat-absorbing substance, available from BBQ stores or hardware stores, every 3–6 months depending upon frequency of use.

Because many BBQs are not covered against fat fires, it is recommended that a proper absorbent product be used. If you don't have any on hand then sand is a good short-term solution.

ROCK TRAY FLAME TAMERS

Flame tamers and ceramic rocks/rock trays are now a more popular option than lava rock, which was a more common choice for many years, but needed to be replaced every 6–12 months, depending upon frequency of use. Generally it is the time to replace the rocks when they can no longer absorb any more fat and are starting to catch fire, and remain on fire.

BURNERS

A light layer of cooking oil can be applied to the burners to help prevent rust; however, due to constant heat this will not have a lasting effect. A wire brush can also be used to clean the burners and prolong the life. 'Protect them from the weather', is the best advice.

HOSE AND REGULATORS

It is important to keep a close eye on these for wear and fraying. If in doubt replace them immediately.

GAS CYLINDER

It is required by law to have all gas cylinders tested and stamped by a licensed gas fitter every 10 years. Large fines may be given for failure to follow safety regulations. Plus it's just common sense. Be sure to check with your gas supplier regarding the current regulations.

IN SUMMARY

To ensure you and your BBQ share a long and trouble-free life, keep your BBQ sheltered from the weather, pay attention to the condition of all parts and fittings and replace immediately if in doubt. Don't be afraid to use lots of cooking oil.

THE RECIPES

You'll see at the top of each recipe we've provided a Beer Rating. This relates to the overall ease of the recipe with 1 being dead simple and 3 being a little more involved. The rating is a rough guide; however, the cooking and preparation times given are quite accurate.

MEASURES FOR SUCCESS

You may find that cooking times vary depending on your barbecue and the weather conditions – for example if it's really windy you may find your barbecue heat fluctuates. For testing the recipes, we used 20ml (4 teaspoon) tablespoon measures; however, if you don't have one of these, the average dessert spoon is just a bit smaller than this, so use one of these and adjust as necessary. Cup measures are standard Australian cup measures (250 ml), not just any old coffee or tea cup you find in your cupboard! But except for the baking recipes, being a bit out here and there really isn't going to make much difference to the recipes.

QUICK AND EASY ON A PLATE!

HONEY AND SOY SAUSAGE BITES

Combine 1 part wholegrain or French mustard to 2 parts honey. Cut good quality sausages into bite-sized pieces and then brush all over with the glaze. Grill on a medium–hot grill for about 5 minutes, turning regularly.

SWEET CHILLI AND LIME SAUSAGES

Combine sweet chilli sauce with a little fresh lime juice and plenty of black pepper. Brush all over sausages and cook over a medium–hot barbecue for about 20 minutes, until cooked-through. Slice into chunks to serve.

Cabanossi, chorizo and pepperoni are also great done on the barbecue, just cut them into shorter lengths then grill for about 5 minutes, until slightly blackened.

GARLIC AND HERB CHICKEN

Combine some olive oil, crushed garlic, black pepper and chopped fresh parsley or coriander. Brush all over bite-sized pieces of chicken thigh, then grill on a medium–hot grill for about 10 minutes, until cooked through, turning occasionally.

QUICK AND EASY ON A PLATE!

CHEESY TRIANGLES

Take a flour tortilla or burrito and spread one side lightly with pesto. Scatter over grated mozzarella or cheddar cheese and chopped green chillies, if liked. Top with a second tortilla or burrito and cook on the plate of a hot barbecue for about 3 minutes, turning carefully once. Serve hot, cut into wedges.

MINI BRUSCETTA

Cut thinish slices on the diagonal from a French stick. Drizzle each side with good-quality olive oil, then cook briefly on each side on a medium–hot barbecue plate, until toasted and a little blackened in places. Rub with half a garlic clove then top with any of the following ideas:

■ sliced cherry tomatoes and fresh basil leaves
■ salami and thin slices of cucumber
■ chargrilled sliced vegetables, such as zucchini, capsicum and eggplant.

GARLIC PITTA FINGERS

Combine good-quality olive oil with some crushed garlic. Wrap pieces of pitta bread individually in foil and cook on a hot barbecue for 5 minutes, turning once. Remove from the foil, brush with the garlic oil and cook on the barbie for about a minute on each side until crisp. Cut into fingers and serve.

MAKE YOUR BEER COLDER
Did you know that adding salt to your iced water keeps your beers even colder?

PRAWNS WITH TEQUILA MAYONNAISE

1 BEER RATING

Peel the prawns as described in the box on the right and put in a bowl. Pour over 2 tablespoons of the tequila and toss about a bit. Set aside.

Using a fork, gradually whisk the remaining tequila (about a shot glass worth) into the mayonnaise, making sure it is well combined, then transfer to a serving dish.

Preheat your barbecue flat plate to high. Place the prawns on the barbecue – being a bit careful as the tequila could ignite – and cook for about 3 minutes, turning once during cooking, until cooked through. Serve immediately accompanied by the mayo for dipping.

PREP: 30 minutes (mostly peeling the prawns)
COOK: 3 minutes
SERVES: 4–6

24 raw medium king prawns
70ml tequila
250g (1 cup) whole-egg mayonnaise

Let us hear your proud grunts of approval for this recipe: tequila is one of those drinks that you love at the time, then it's put back on the shelf for a few more months. The addition of tequila prawns to your BBQ adds the same excitement, all without the next day sorrows of the Tequila Sunrise or Margarita.

These prawns are guaranteed to be a talking point amongst your mates at your next BBQ.

GO THE RAW PRAWN
It is preferable to buy prawns with the shells on and then peel them yourself. However, if you really can't be bothered then buy raw, peeled prawns. Do not buy peeled cooked prawns if you intend to barbecue them. However, if you want a quick snack or entrée, then you could buy cooked prawns and just make the mayonnaise.

HOW TO PEEL PRAWNS
To peel the prawns, first pull off the head by giving it a firm tug. Then, leaving the tail on, peel off the shell and legs – they should come off quite easily. Using a sharp knife, make a shallow slit down the back and pull out the intestinal vein that runs down to the tail. Rinse under cold water. Done.

TOP TIP
Any left-over mayonnaise is great in burgers, with hot chips and for using as a dip for other seafood and meat.

SPICY PORK RIBS

1 BEER RATING

Combine all the ingredients except the ribs and make sure it is well mixed. If your ribs are still in one piece, separate them by slicing in between the bones. Put them in a shallow dish and pour the marinade over. Turn the ribs to coat them, using your hands to massage the mixture into the ribs well. Leave to marinate in the fridge for at least 2 hours and for up to 48 hours but do not remove stubbies to allow room for the dish. Take other food out – beer needs to be cold and on hand at all times.

Once marinated, drain the marinade into a small saucepan and bring to the boil.

Preheat the barbecue to a medium heat, lightly oil the barbecue plate and cook the ribs for 30–35 minutes (depending on size), turning regularly until they are tender and cooked through and slightly blackened on the outside, basting with the boiled marinade several times during cooking. Serve with lots of cold beer.

MUST BE COOKED UNDER A HOODED OR KETTLE BARBECUE

PREP: 10 minutes (plus 2-28 hours marinating)
COOK: 30 minutes
SERVES: 4ish

4 tablespoons (⅓ cup) soy sauce
3 tablespoons (¼ cup) rice vinegar or white wine vinegar
4 garlic cloves, crushed
2.5cm knob of fresh ginger, peeled and finely grated
2 teaspoons chilli powder
2 tablespoons honey
2 tablespoons wholegrain mustard
About 1.25kg American-style pork ribs (ask your butcher to separate the ribs)

TOP TIP
These are very messy to eat so put out lots of napkins or paper towel.

BARBECUED KING PRAWNS
TWO OPTIONS - SWEET CHILLI OR GARLIC

2 BEER RATING

As well as two flavouring options, you've also got two options for preparing the prawns. Both are butterflied but one way keeps the shell on and the other removes it. With the shells off you have perfect beer finger food and peeling increases the surface area of the prawn for the marinade and there's no fuss or mess with the shells. However, with the shells on your job is easier as you don't have to peel them completely. It also keeps them a bit moister when cooking. The decision is yours – or do them half and half. Either way you need to pull off the heads.

If peeling completely, once you've removed the head, pull off the shell, leaving the tail intact, then slice down the back and remove the vein. Turn over and slice the down the belly, but not all the way through to butterfly (flatten). Rinse and pat dry – they are now ready for marinating.

If leaving the shells on, once you've removed the head, turn the prawn over and slice through the back shell. Remove the intestine, then turn over and press down on the back to butterfly the prawn. Rinse under cold water and pat dry.

Put the prawns in a bowl and add either the sweet chilli sauce or the oil and garlic. Either way season them with salt and pepper.

Preheat the barbecue to high and cook on an oiled hotplate for a few sips of beer on both sides – 2 or 3 minutes all up. Supply loads of paper napkins and, if you're feeling posh, finger bowls for washing sticky fingers.

PREP: 10–30 minutes. depending on if you are peeling prawns or not
COOK: 2–3 minutes
SERVES: 4–6

24 raw king prawns (or as many as you like, allow about 5–6 per person)
Salt and pepper

CHILLI PRAWNS:
2 tablespoons sweet chilli sauce

GARLIC PRAWNS:
4 tablespoons olive oil
4 garlic cloves (finely chopped)

WHY BARBECUING IS BETTER THAN SEX!

- You can BBQ outdoors without getting arrested.
- Your good-looking neighbour is more likely to say yes to a BBQ.
- BBQs heat up at the flick of a switch.
- If the cling wrap breaks, your food doesn't multiply.
- Chipolatas are an ideal size for a BBQ snack.

PORK KEBABS WITH HERBY MAYO

1 BEER RATING

If using wooden skewers, soak them in water for about an hour, or for at least as long as it takes to make the kebabs, to prevent them burning on the barbecue.

Squeeze the juice from 1 lemon and combine with the oil and garlic and add a good grinding of black pepper. Put the pork in a bowl and pour over the marinade. Toss well and leave to marinate in the fridge for 30 minutes if you've got time, or for a few hours if that suits you better.

Meanwhile, combine the coriander mayo ingredients, put in a serving dish and chill until needed.

Thread the pork onto the kebabs, adding a couple of wedges of onion (if using) to each kebab.

Preheat the barbecue to medium and cook the kebabs for about 10 minutes, turning halfway through, or until just cooked through and brown on the outside. Cut the remaining lemon into wedges and squeeze a couple of wedges worth of juice over the kebabs just before serving. Serve accompanied by the mayo and the remaining lemon wedges.

PREP: 20 minutes (plus optional 30 minutes marinating)
COOK: about 10 minutes
MAKES: 12 kebabs

12 wooden or metal skewers
2 lemons
2 tablespoons olive oil
1 garlic clove, crushed
Black pepper
800g pork neck fillet, cut into 2–3cm cubes
3 small red onions, cut into 8 wedges each (optional)

CORIANDER MAYO
250g (1 cup) good quality whole-egg mayonnaise
1 garlic clove, crushed (optional)
2 tablespoons chopped fresh coriander leaves

TOP TIP

You could also use parsley, basil or chives, but they do need to be fresh, definitely not dried.

THE 60-SECOND GUIDE TO BARBECUING

THE ESSENTIALS:
- ■ Beer in ice/fridge
- ■ Wine and soft drink
- ■ Friends/mates
- ■ BBQ and fuel
- ■ Cooking oil
- ■ Utensils – scraper and tongs
- ■ Lots of meat
- ■ Sauces for meat
- ■ Second-hand cricket bat and worn tennis ball
- ■ TV or radio for the sport

EVERYTHING ELSE IS OPTIONAL:
- ■ Tables and chairs
- ■ Plates and cutlery
- ■ Bread and salad – some people like this to accompany meat
- ■ Snack products such as chips and dips
- ■ Back-up beer and meat
- ■ Music
- ■ Hat and sunscreen
- ■ Frisbee
- ■ Citronella candles and bug repellent
- ■ Torch and/or outdoor lights

CHILLI AND COCONUT MARINATED PRAWNS

1 BEER RATING

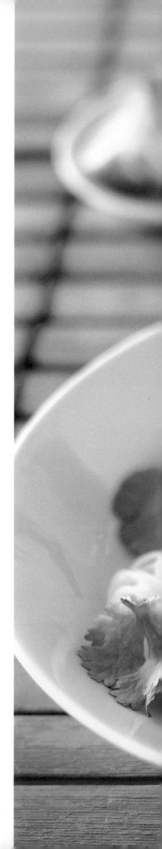

Combine the coconut milk, chilli, soy sauce and coriander and put into a medium-sized bowl. Peel the prawns as in the box on the right and add to the bowl. Mix everything together well and leave to marinate for about an hour, if possible.

Preheat your barbecue flat plate to high. Remove the prawns from the marinade, allowing any excess to drip off. Place the prawns on the barbecue and cook for about 3 minutes, turning once during cooking and squeezing with some lime while cooking, until cooked through. Serve immediately.

PREP: 30 minutes, mostly peeling the prawns (plus 1 hour marinating, optional)
COOK: about 3 minutes
SERVES: 4–6

200ml can coconut milk
1 small red chilli, seeded and finely chopped (remember to thoroughly wash your hands and the utensils after doing this)
1 tablespoon soy sauce (optional)
2 tablespoons chopped fresh coriander
24 raw medium king prawns
1 lime, halved

TOP TIP #1
It is preferable to buy prawns with the shells on and then peel them yourself. However, if you really can't be bothered then buy raw, peeled prawns. Do not buy peeled cooked prawns.

TOP TIP #2
To peel the prawns, first pull off the head giving it a firm tug. Then, leaving the tail on, peel off the shell and legs – they should come off quite easily. Using a sharp knife, make a shallow slit down the back and pull out the intestinal vein that runs down to the tail. Rinse under cold water. Done.

NOODLE SALAD
These prawns are great served on a noodle salad. To serve 4, simply soak 300g rice vermicelli noodles for 5–7 minutes in boiling water. Drain well then stir in the juice of 1 lime, 2 tablespoons olive oil, 1 chopped small red chilli, a handful of coriander leaves and a handful of mint leaves (torn if large) and season with salt and pepper. Toss it all together well and set aside until ready.

PORTUGUESE CHILLI CHICKEN BURGER

2 BEER RATING

Put each chicken fillet on a chopping board and cover with a piece of cling wrap or greaseproof paper, then flatten to about half the thickness with a meat mallet, rolling pin, or brick if that's all you've got! Cut in two, so you end up with two flat pieces.

Combine the sweet chilli sauce, lime juice, garlic and chilli. Put the chicken in a shallow dish and pour the sauce over it, turning to coat. If you've got time, leave this to marinate in the fridge, remembering to bring it to room temperature before you start to cook.

Preheat the barbecue to medium–low and brush with oil. Add the chicken and cook for about 6–7 minutes on each side, or until cooked through, brushing once with the marinade just before you turn them over. Season the chicken with salt and pepper once it is cooked.

Cook the buns on the cut side only for 30 seconds, spread with mayonnaise and extra chilli sauce, then top with lettuce and chicken.

PREP: 15 minutes (plus time to marinate if desired)
COOK: about 15 minutes
MAKES: 4 burgers

4 large skinless, chicken thigh fillets
3 tablespoons (¼ cup) sweet chilli sauce, plus extra to serve
3 tablespoons (¼ cup) lime juice
2 garlic cloves, crushed
1 small (bird's eye) red chilli, halved, seeded and finely chopped
Salt and pepper
4 sesame seed buns, split
Mayonnaise
Crispy lettuce leaves

TOP TIP #1

When brushing meat that is cooking with a marinade, you need to be aware of food poisoning risks. Basically only brush the meat if it is going to be cooked well again on the part that is brushed to kill any bacteria that could be transferred from the marinade to the meat. To prevent this problem, boil the marinade before using it again as a baste.

TOP TIP #2

You can also use chicken breast for the burgers, although they are not as juicy as a thigh fillet. Cook for slightly less time.

WHY BARBECUING IS BETTER THAN SEX!

- ■ Gauges are available to let you know when you're going to run out of gas.
- ■ You can wear thongs, drink beer and watch sport at the same time.
- ■ Your BBQ doesn't get offended when your mates turn up unannounced.
- ■ Large groups are welcome at a BBQ.

BARBECUE PIZZA

2 BEER RATING

The pizzas need to be cooked over an indirect heat, but in order to get the base crispy you need to preheat the main flat plate as well and then turn it off after a few minutes of cooking so the base doesn't just blacken and burn. Firstly, remove the two plates covering your two side burners then preheat the whole barbecue to hot with the hood down.

With a coal barbecue preheat the coals for about 45 minutes, then just before you put the pizza on, put a baking tray on the coals under the grill.

Cover the pizza bases with tomato sauce, then top with the mozzarella, capsicum, cabanossi and ham. Season with salt and pepper. Once the barbecue is up to around 200°C, put one pizza on the flat plate and replace the hood. After 2 minutes turn off the flat plate and leave to cook with the hood down for about 20 minutes, until the cheese melts and the base is golden, not blackened! If cooking the other pizza straight away give the hot plate a good blast of heat for a few minutes before putting the second one on.

MUST BE COOKED ON A HOODED OR KETTLE BARBECUE

This recipe makes two pizzas but for best results you can really only cook one at a time.

PREP: 15 minutes
COOK: about 20 minutes
MAKES: 2 big pizzas

2 large pizza bases
250g jar tomato pasta sauce
250g grated mozzarella cheese
200g roasted red capsicums, chopped
1–2 cabanossi, sliced
150g thickly sliced ham, chopped
Salt and pepper

WHY BARBECUING IS BETTER THAN SEX!

- You can tell your mum about your new job selling BBQs.
- You can look your neighbours in the eyes when you apologise for your loud, late-night BBQs.
- If a BBQ fizzles out you can always blame the weather.
- Having a BBQ by yourself will not send you blind.

TOP TIP #1
Other toppings that you can use include: jars of antipasto; sliced mushrooms and chargrilled eggplant. Sliced tomato, chargrilled zucchini or crumbled goats' cheese.

TOP TIP #2
Toppings that can be thrown on once the pizza is cooked include a handful of rocket leaves, shavings of parmesan cheese, chopped avocado or toasted pine nuts. Get creative. Just make sure any meat you use is cooked and heated through before serving.

ROAST CHOOK

3 BEER RATING

Use an indirect heat to cook the chicken so it doesn't just blacken underneath. To do this, heat all the burners on your hooded barbecue to medium–hot. If using a coal barbie, heat the coals for about 45 minutes then put a baking tray on top, but under the grill rack.

Wash the chicken inside and out and pat dry with paper towel. Combine the butter, herbs and a good grinding of salt and pepper in a small bowl. Using your fingers, carefully separate the skin from the breast meat (the bit on the top of the chicken that slopes down), being careful not to break the skin. Then carefully stuff the butter under the skin, smoothing it out by smoothing the skin from on the top. If you have trouble with this, then melt the butter, add the herbs and seasoning and then about 10 minutes before the end of cooking, brush or spoon this all over the chicken a couple of times. Either way, you should brush the chicken all over with some of the oil before you start to cook it.

If using a gas barbie, brush the centre plate with oil, then turn off the heat under this plate only. Sit the chicken on the centre plate and if using a coal barbie sit the chicken on the grill. Cover with the hood and cook (breast side up) for about 1 hour 10 minutes.

About 20 minutes before the chook is cooked, toss the potato slices in olive oil and arrange around the chicken. Cook on both sides until they are tender and golden. Halfway through cooking, squeeze a little lemon over the potatoes.

To check if the chicken is cooked through – this is very important so as not to kill anyone from salmonella food poisoning – pierce a thigh and press it so that the juices come out. If there is any trace of pink (i.e. blood), cook it a little longer, but if the juices are completely clear then it is cooked. Remove the chicken from the heat and, if you've got time, sit it on a plate next to the barbecue where it is still a bit warm and cover with foil. Leave it there for about 10 minutes before carving and serving with the potatoes and with the wedges of lemon for squeezing over the chicken. Sprinkle sea salt over the potatoes just before serving.

MUST BE COOKED UNDER A HOODED OR KETTLE BARBECUE

PREP: 15 minutes
COOK: 1 hour 10 minutes
SERVES: 4

1.8kg chicken
75g butter, softened but not melted
2 tablespoons chopped fresh flat-leaf parsley, coriander or basil, finely chopped
salt and pepper
2–3 tablespoons olive oil
1kg waxy potatoes, such as chat, pink fir apple or kipfler, scrubbed and thinly sliced. Five mm is a good thickness.
1 lemon, cut into wedges
1–2 teaspoons sea salt

TOPICS TO DEBATE AT A BBQ

- Why barbequing is better than sex.
- Why you and your best mates could destroy any world class women's sporting team and what prize you would claim for winning.
- Which is better, Ford or Holden, including real life Bathurst examples.
- Which superhero would win, stating reasons why.
- Who can name the most Seinfeld episodes.

TOP TIP #1
For ease of cooking the chicken and cleaning the barbie afterwards, you may want to cook the chicken and potatoes in one or two of those disposable aluminium trays.

TOP TIP #2
If you don't want to make the potatoes, just serve your fave potato salad or some boiled spuds.

BUTTERFLIED LEG OF LAMB

2 BEER RATING

If you remember, you might want to get this ready the day before. This will not only help the lamb develop a great flavour from the marinade but it also means you have more time to do the important jobs, like chilling the beers and having a drink or two with your mates.

If the butcher has not done so already, take a rolling pin to your leg of lamb and bash it a few times on the thickest point on the cut side of the meat to even out the thickness a little. Then make a couple of quite thick slashes through the thickest part of the meat to help the heat penetrate evenly.

Put the meat on a large plate or shallow dish. Combine the remaining ingredients, the except the garlic, and rub all over the meat on both sides, with your hands. Then also on the cut side of the meat, make a few shallow cuts (about 10 or so) at random and then stick a slice of garlic into each slit.

Preferably leave to marinate in the fridge for up to 24 hours; if you don't have time, no worries, just start cooking. However, if you do marinate it, try to bring it back to room temperature for about 20 minutes before you BBQ it so it cooks more quickly and evenly.

Get your barbecue to a medium heat – too hot and the meat will just char on the outside and remain raw in the middle – and add the meat (cut side down). Cook for about 15 minutes, then turn over and cook with the hood down for a further 15 minutes until both sides are crusty and dark brown. If you don't have a hood, no worries, just cook it for about 15 minutes, or until done to your liking – stick a sharp knife into the middle and see – if it's still too pink and translucent cook it for a little longer, maybe turning down the heat so it doesn't just burn on the outside.

Remove the meat from the barbecue and sit it on a plate by the side of the barbie (where it is a bit warm) covered with a sheet of foil, for about 10 minutes. This will make for a much more succulent meal, as the juices will be drawn back into the meat, rather than onto the plate when you carve it. Again if you don't have time, just serve it, maybe with some crusty bread for mopping up the juices.

IT IS PREFERABLE TO COOK THIS UNDER A HOODED BBQ

PREP: 10 minutes (plus overnight marinating, optional)
COOK: about 30 minutes
SERVES: 8–10

2.5kg leg of lamb, butterflied (get your butcher to do this for you, 2.5kg is the weight including the bones, it will be about 1.9kg without)
4 tablespoons olive oil
1 teaspoon ground coriander
1 teaspoon ground cumin
1 teaspoon ground chilli
5cm knob of fresh ginger, peeled and finely grated
Salt and pepper
1 large garlic clove, thinly sliced

TOP TIP #1

If you are going to rest your meat after cooking (see end of recipe), then it will continue to cook a bit during this time, so it's best to pull it off while still a little pink in the centre.

TOPICS TO DEBATE AT A BBQ

- If a tree falls in the woods and no one is around to hear it, does anyone really care?
- All time favourite car chase scenes.
- What is the best football code, which is the fittest code, who wears the smallest shorts and should a field goal be worth 1 or 3 points?
- Who has the most annoying sayings out of your boss and your ex-girlfriend?
- Name as many sports as possible which require no athletic ability.

ROAST PORK AND VEGGIES

3 BEER RATING

You really do need indirect heat to cook the pork. So heat all the burners on your hooded barbecue to medium. If using a coal barbie, heat the coals for about 45 minutes then, just before you put the pork and vegetables on, put a baking tray on top of the coals, but under the grill rack.

If your pork hasn't already been scored in a diamond pattern, do this all over the skin. Rub the sea salt into the skin. Combine the oil and garlic with plenty of salt and pepper. Put the vegetables in a large bowl and toss them in the oil mixture.

Put the pork in the centre of the barbie (on a flat plate if you have one) and surround with the vegetables. Turn off the centre plate heat, cover with the hood and roast for 1 hour 10 – 1 hour 20 minutes. Turn the vegetables over occasionally to ensure they do not blacken and that they all cook evenly.

After 1 hour 10 minutes check that the pork is cooked by sticking a skewer into the thickest part – the juices should run clear. If not, cook it for an extra 10 minutes, but do not overcook it or it will become dry. Remove the pork from the heat and sit it on a plate next to the barbecue where it is still a bit warm and cover with foil. Leave it there for about 10 minutes before carving into individual ribs and serving with the vegetables.

MUST BE COOKED UNDER A HOODED OR KETTLE BARBECUE

PREP: 20 minutes
COOK: 1 hour 10 – 1 hour 20 minutes
SERVES: 6

1 rack of pork with 6 ribs (ask your butcher to remove the chine bone to make carving easy and to score the skin in a diamond pattern)
1 tablespoon sea salt
3 tablespoons (¼ cup) olive oil
2 garlic cloves, crushed
Salt and pepper
2 red onions, cut into thick wedges
1.2–1.5kg piece pumpkin, cut into wedges
5 large potatoes, scrubbed and cut into chunks

TOPICS TO DEBATE AT A BBQ

- Best sportsperson ever
- Did man really land on the moon?
- What you would do if you were invisible for a day
- In soccer, if you get caught 'taking a dive' by the referee what should the penalty be?
- Volvo drivers … enough said
- Is it ok to date co-workers?
- What's more important, your BBQ or your thumbs.

ROAST BEEF

2 BEER RATING

Combine the chilli flakes, pepper, honey, coriander seeds and olive oil in a small bowl and mix well. Smear all over the beef and set aside. As with so many marinated meats this will be really helped by a substantial marinating time – preferably overnight in the fridge. If you have time to do this, remember to bring it to room temperature before barbecuing, so it cooks more quickly and evenly. However, if you don't have time (although even 30 minutes would help) you can cook it straight away.

Combine all the mustard condiment ingredients and place in a small serving dish.

Ideally, you want an indirect heat to cook the beef so it doesn't just blacken underneath. If using a gas barbie, heat all the burners to medium–hot then sit the beef on the grill plate between the side burners and turn off the flat plate heat. If using a coal barbie, heat the coals for about 45 minutes then put a baking tray on top of them, but under the grill rack. Sit the beef directly on the grill rack. Cover with the hood and cook for about 50 minutes for juicy and rare meat, for another 10 minutes for medium, or for even longer until cooked to your liking.

If you've got time, transfer the beef to a plate next to the barbecue where it is still a bit warm and cover with foil. Leave it there for about 10 minutes before slicing and serving with the mustard sauce.

TOP TIP #1
If you can't be bothered to make the mustard sauce that's fine, although it's pretty good. Just serve some damned fine Dijon on the side.

TOP TIP #2
This crust is also great on a leg of lamb or lamb cutlets, a loin of pork, or on chicken thighs or legs.

TOP TIP #3
If you want to make to make this for fewer people you'll need about 1.2kg for 6 people and just under 1kg for 4. Keep the rest of the ingredients the same so you have plenty of rub and plenty of sauce. Cook for less time.

TOP TIP #4
Horseradish and creamed horseradish are available from the condiment aisle of the supermarket, near the mustard and stuff. Creamed horseradish is just a bit milder than straight horseradish.

MUST BE COOKED UNDER A HOODED OR KETTLE BARBECUE

PREP: 10 minutes (plus optional 30 minutes–24 hours marinating)
COOK: 50 minutes*
SERVES: 8

1 teaspoon chilli flakes
½ teaspoon black pepper
1 tablespoon honey
1 tablespoon coriander seeds, crushed (optional)
3 tablespoons (¼ cup) olive oil
1.5kg piece beef eye fillet, tied (ask your butcher to do this)

MUSTARD SAUCE:
4 tablespoons (1/3 cup) mayonnaise
2 tablespoons French/Dijon mustard
2 teaspoons grated horseradish or
1 tablespoon creamed horseradish
2 tablespoons lemon juice
Salt and pepper
1–2 teaspoons sea salt

* Note that cooking time depends on how well-done you like you beef. 50 minutes is for medium.

GOOD BOY ...

OH OH! ...

TOO TASTY ...

SIZE MATTERS

Whether size really matters is a question that has been posed throughout the ages, bringing fear and doubt into the minds of all men.

YOU MAY WANT TO GRAB another beer and ensure you're sufficiently relaxed before facing the harsh realities revealed on this page.

Some will argue they only have a small one because of factors outside their control such as 'I really don't get the chance to use it very often', or they will claim 'you can still get the same effect from a smaller one but it just takes more time'. I pity these fools.

When it comes down to it, we all know the answer to this question. Take a look deep down into your soul and there's no escaping the fact: size really does matter.

However, the upside is, unless you already own a BBQ you get to choose how big you want it to be. I'd recommend at least a four burner. If only we had a say in all matters relating to size such as bigger salary, bigger car, bigger house, bigger … well you know what I'm leading to.

Generally, BBQs come in

either three, four or five burner sizes. Three burners are generally 26" but to be extremely confusing are sometimes 31". Four burners are generally 31" with five burners an extreme 39". There are bigger BBQs available but I'm not going to mention them because it makes me jealous.

Remember, when considering what size BBQ to buy you can always turn a burner off if you don't need it, however, you can't increase the cooking surface on those occasions when unexpected friends drop in. Also, when you convert from normal direct heat barbequing to indirect roasting you automatically lose about half the cooking surface (see the chapter: Covered Cooking Down Under).

Therefore, don't skimp on space unless you want to live each day with regret, knowing you really should have got the bigger one. Remember, size really does matter!

JUMBO BEEF BURGERS

Combine all the patty ingredients except the cheese in a bowl and, using your hands, make sure everything is mixed really well together. Divide the mixture into four and shape into balls. Cut four 1cm square pieces of mozzarella from the block and push a square into the center of each ball, pressing the mince back over the hole to cover the cheese. Shape the balls into flattish patties. Chill for 30 minutes. Thinly slice the remaining cheese.

Heat your barbecue to high and cook the patties on each side for 5-6 minutes or until cooked through. Put a slice of cheese onto each patty for the final 2 minutes of cooking so it melts.

Put the burger buns (cut side down) on the BBQ and toast for about 30 seconds. Top each base with some lettuce, tomato and a patty. Add the lid of the bun and serve accompanied by loads of tomato sauce.

PREP: 20 minutes (plus 30 minutes to chill)
COOK: 6 minutes
MAKES: 4 burgers

PATTIES
500g beef mince
2 garlic cloves, crushed
1 small red onion, finely chopped
1 tablespoon tomato paste (optional)
2 tablespoons finely chopped fresh basil
Salt and pepper
About 100g block mozzarella cheese

4 burger buns, halved
A few crunchy lettuce leaves
2 ripe tomatoes, sliced
Tomato sauce and/or other condiments

TOP TIP #1
If you don't want to stuff the patties with cheese you don't have to. They will work and taste just fine.

TOP TIP #2
If you prefer to make smaller burgers, then it's easy to make 6-8, just cut a few extra squares and slices of cheese and cook for slightly less time.

WHY BARBECUING IS BETTER THAN SEX!

- If you have two different BBQs in the one week no-one gets upset.
- Ring burners are cheaper than diamond rings.
- The BBQ never gets a headache.
- There are instruction manuals to tell you what is wrong with your BBQ.

CHICKEN TIKKA KEBABS WITH CUCUMBER DIP

2 BEER RATING

If using wooden skewers, soak them in water for an hour, or for at least as long as it takes to make the kebabs, to prevent them burning on the barbecue.

To make the kebabs, combine all the ingredients, except the chicken, and mix well. Add the chicken and mix everything together well, using your hands so the chicken is well coated. Leave to marinate for an hour if you've got time or overnight in the fridge if you're that well organized.

To make the cucumber dip, halve the cucumber lengthways then use a teaspoon to scoop out the seeds. Chop the flesh finely. Put the yoghurt in a bowl and give it a bit of a beating to make sure it is smooth, then stir in the cucumber, garlic and chilli. Chill until needed.

Once the chicken has marinated, skewer 5 pieces onto each skewer.

Heat your barbecue to medium heat and if possible put two bricks or other non-flammable items just less than a skewer-length apart on the barbecue so you can rest the kebabs above the grill. If you can't do this never mind, but you might find that the kebabs stick a bit. Cook the kebabs for about 30 minutes, turning regularly until cooked through. They will cook much quicker if they are directly on the grill, but be careful not to overcook them as they will dry out.

Wrap the naan bread in foil and cook on each side side for 4–5 minutes. Serve the kebabs with the cucumber dip and naan bread alongside.

PREP: 15–20 minutes
COOK: about 30 minutes
MAKES: 8 kebabs

250g (1 cup) Greek-style natural yoghurt
1 teaspoon lemon juice
2.5cm knob of fresh ginger, finely grated
1 teaspoon ground cardamom
½ teaspoon ground cumin or ground coriander
1 teaspoon paprika
750g skinless, chicken breasts, cut into 2–3cm cubes

CUCUMBER YOGHURT DIP:
1 Lebanese cucumber
250g (1 cup) Greek-style natural yoghurt
1 small garlic clove, crushed
1 small green chilli, seeded and finely chopped

2–4 naan bread, to serve
8 metal or wooden skewers

TOPICS TO DEBATE AT A BBQ

- Do aliens exist and, if so, what's the whole probing thing about?
- Whether real men actually drink cider.
- Who is the sexiest woman in the world.
- Merits of sports you can play while drinking a schooner.
- Reasons why it was better to live in the 1800s than the current day.

STEAK SANDWICHES WITH BALSAMIC ONIONS

Heat the barbecue flat plate and chargrill plate to medium-high.

To make the relish, toss the onion slices in the oil to coat. Spread them out on the barbecue flat plate and cook for about 10 minutes, moving them regularly so they don't burn. Scoop them into a small pile and pour the balsamic vinegar and sugar over them, mix, then cook for another couple of minutes. Transfer to a bowl.

Get the chargrill plate really hot, then brush each steak with oil and cook for 1–1½ minutes on each side for medium rare and for an extra minute each side for well done. Transfer to a warm plate and season with salt and pepper.

Toast the bread on both sides for about 30 seconds, until warmed through. Put some greenery on the bread, top with a steak then spoon some onions on top and serve.

PREP: 10 minutes
COOK: about 15 minutes
SERVES: 4

4 x 150g thin steaks (or enough for however many people you've got turning up)
Salt and pepper
A loaf of good quality bread, like sourdough or Italian, sliced
Some rocket or lettuce (optional)

BALSAMIC ONION RELISH:
2 large onions, thinly sliced
1 tablespoon olive oil
1 tablespoon balsamic vinegar
2 teaspoons sugar

TOP TIP #1
The best steaks for barbecuing are rump, sirloin and fillet. A particularly quick cooking steak is a minute steak from the upper part of a sirloin. You could also use New York steaks, halved horizontally.

TOP TIP #2
Although it won't be quite the same, if you haven't got any balsamic vinegar, splash a bit of beer on the onions instead of the vinegar – it will sweeten them up a little.

TOP TIP #3
If your loaf is quite small, slice on the diagonal to make larger slices.

BASIC STEAK
Before cooking, apply good-quality cooking oil to a plate or grill which should be very hot.
Place the meat on the hooded barbecue and leave until the juices rise to the top, then turn over (only once) and leave until cooked to your liking – rare, medium, well-done (if you must). If you have a hooded barbecue, close the hood in between turning.
A tip for nicely chargrilled steak on the outside but juicy and tender on the inside: take directly from the freezer, make sure the barbeque is preheated and throw straight on the heat. It takes longer to cook, allowing more time in your backyard with your mates. A win-win situation.

LAMB CUTLETS MARINATED IN YOGHURT AND CHUTNEY

1 BEER RATING

Cut the lemon into eight wedges and squeeze the juice from two into a bowl. Add the yoghurt and chutney, a good pinch of salt and a good grinding of black pepper. Stir well. Put the cutlets in a shallow dish and spoon over the marinade. Rub in well and leave to marinate in the fridge for an hour, if possible.

Take your meat out of the fridge to come to room temperature. Preheat the chargrill racks on your barbecue to high heat. Add the cutlets and cook for 1–2 minutes on each side for rare or a little longer if you prefer your meat more cooked.

Serve with the remaining wedges of lemon, a green salad and bread.

PREP: Less than 10 minutes (plus 1 hour marinating, optional)
COOK: 3–4 minutes
SERVES: 4 (makes 12 cutlets)

1 lemon
250g (1 cup) Greek-style or natural yoghurt
3 tablespoons mango chutney
Sea salt (preferably) and black pepper
12 lamb cutlets

TOP TIP #1
To get more juice out of your lemon before juicing, roll it backwards and forwards a few times on the kitchen counter, pushing down quite firmly.

TOP TIP #2
If there's one (more) tip I can give you before cooking these cutlets for the first time it would have to be, cook a double serving. These cutlets will challenge your own favourite lamb dish. They're quick, super tasty and, because of the lemon and yoghurt, they are so tender and have the most amazing texture when cooked.

Be sure to bring out these bad boys if your mates challenge you to a BBQ cook-off or if you are looking to impress a new date at your BBQ.

BABY OCTOPUS SALAD

3 BEER RATING

If you couldn't buy cleaned octopus, you'll need to clean the guts out. Grab a beer for your octopus anatomy lesson. Even if you've bought cleaned octopus there's still a bit of preparation that needs to be done.

First off use a sharp knife to cut between the head and the tentacle section, just below the eyes. Then cut the tentacles in half longthways and pull off the beak-thing. Rinse the tentacles under cold water, pulling off the skin – this can be a little difficult to do but it must be done. Snip the tips off the tentacles and, if the octopuses are particularly large, cut the tentacles in half again. Now, back to the head/body. Make a careful slit down one side of the body – trying to avoid the ink sac – and scrape out all the insides, including the ink sac. Rinse under cold water.

Remove the eyes by slicing off a thin disc and discarding. Then pull off the thin skin, once again under running water. Then cut the head in half. OK, you are ready to go.

Combine the soy sauce, vegetable oil and hoisin sauce and pour over the octopus. Leave to marinate for about 30 minutes.

Preheat your barbecue plate to medium heat. Remove the octopus from the marinade and cook for 2–3 minutes or until they are cooked through and curly. Squeeze a little lime juice over then serve just like this with lime wedges to accompany or on one of the salad options.

PREP: 30–40 minutes (plus 1 hour marinating, optional)
COOK: 2–3 minutes
SERVES: 6

1kg baby octopus, preferably cleaned (ask your fishmonger to do this)
3 tablespoons (¼ cup) light soy sauce
1 tablespoon vegetable oil
1 tablespoon hoisin sauce
1 lime, cut into wedges
Salad, to serve (optional)

SIMPLE LEAF SALAD

Combine a couple of handfuls rocket and a couple handfuls of crunchy lettuce. Add a little olive oil, white wine vinegar, salt and pepper and toss together.

ASIAN SALAD

Combine 3 or 4 handfuls mizuna salad leaves or a bag or two Asian salad leaves with a good handful of snow pea sprouts and a Lebanese cucumber cut into matchsticks. Combine 2 tablespoons of vegetable oil with 1 tablespoon of lime juice and 1 teaspoon of sesame oil and use to dress the salad.

WHY BARBECUING IS BETTER THAN SEX!

- ☐ You don't have to shower between footy and the BBQ.
- ☐ You can BBQ all day, every day.
- ☐ You can be ugly as sin and still have regular BBQs.
- ☐ A BBQ is cheaper than a three-course dinner, wine and a movie.
- ☐ Don't get me started on Valentine's Day.
- ☐ BBQ trolleys are always hardwood.

WHOLE BARBECUED FISH

2 BEER RATING

Make four double layered pieces of aluminium foil, large enough to completely enclose each fish. Brush the foil with oil so the fish doesn't stick. Spread a big spoonful of sauce down the centre of the foil, then put a fish on top and paint inside and out with more sauce. Place the onion rings inside and out, add a good sprinkling of cracked pepper and sea salt and completely enclose the fish.

Preheat your barbeque to medium and place the fish directly on the hot plate or grill. Cook the fish for 5 minutes then, carefully, using a fish slice, or similar, turn the fish over and cook for a further 5 or so minutes. Carefully open the foil and check if it is cooked. It should flake easily, if not cook it for a minute or two longer.

MUST BE COOKED UNDER A HOODED OR KETTLE BARBECUE

PREP: 15 minutes
COOK: 10–15 minutes
SERVES: 4

1 tablespoon vegetable or olive oil
250g jar tomato pasta sauce
4 whole fish (about 350-400g each), such as tailor, small snapper or whiting, scaled and gutted
1 onion, sliced
Freshly ground black pepper and sea salt
Lime wedges, to serve, optional

TOP TIP

This is great camping food. You can cook any fish you've caught, once you've scaled and gutted them. If they are particularly small fish, serve 2 per person. You can also cook one large fish (about 2kg) this way. It will take about 10 minutes on each side.

CRISPY SALMON STEAKS

1 BEER RATING

Combine all the ingredients, except the salmon, and mix well, ensuring the honey has dissolved. Put the salmon in a shallow dish and pour over the marinade. Turn to coat the steaks and leave to marinate in the fridge for 30 minutes or longer if you want.

Preheat your BBQ chargrill plate to medium–high. Remove the salmon from the marinade, allowing any excess to drip off, and cook (skin-side up) for 2–3 minutes. Turn over and cook for a further 2 minutes or until they are still just a little bit under-cooked in the middle. Sit in a warm place for a couple of minutes before serving.

MMMMMMH ...

PREP: 10 minutes (plus 30 minutes marinating, optional)
COOK: 5 minutes
SERVES: 4

3 tablespoons (¼ cup) soy sauce
3 tablespoons (¼ cup) honey
1 tablespoon vegetable oil
1 tablespoon oyster sauce
1 garlic clove, crushed
1 tablespoon wholegrain mustard
4 medium sized skin-on salmon fillet steaks
1 large cos lettuce, leaves separated, to serve (or other salad)
Salad dressing, to serve

TOP TIP
This recipe is easy to make for more people, just increase the ingredients accordingly.

QUICK 3-LEAF SALAD
Combine all the separated lettuce leaves from 1 baby cos lettuce, 1 oak lettuce and 1 radiccio lettuce in a serving bowl and dress with your choice of dressing.

QUICK SALAD DRESSING
Combine 1 tablespoon wholegrain mustard, 2 tablespoons lemon juice and 80ml (1/3 cup) olive oil. Pour over salad, toss and serve.

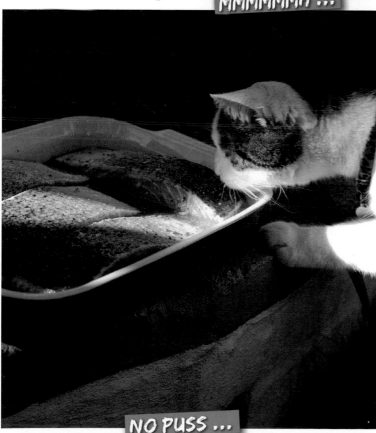

NO PUSS ...

BUSTED!

COW CUTS

Dogs are a man's best friend, but when it comes to Real Men barbecuing, cows come in a close second.

At a BBQ, cows not only supply the delicious meat, but also the spread for buttering our steak sangers. If only we could find a way for cows to also make bread and chill beer. Although … the fact that they don't is probably a good thing. Local councils would not look too kindly on all Aussie blokes having cattle in their backyards, just in case unannounced friends drop in for a BBQ.

If you doubt blokes would go to this extent for the perfect BBQ, just check out the meat section of the supermarket. Watch the bright excited eyes of real men light up as they take in the endless BBQ meat opportunities on offer.

It's important we're educated about where all our favourite cuts of meat come from, as it's a part of our Aussie BBQ culture. Cows and the endless BBQ products they provide has helped shape who we are today. Imagine a BBQ without steak? Imagine an Aussie without a BBQ?

A big thank you goes out to the farmers who keep nice green pastures and the cows fed, despite the droughts, working hard to ensure the BBQ lifestyle in Australia lives on.

NECK

RIB SET/
BEEF CUTLETS

CHUCK

BLADE

BRISKET

SHORT RIBS

The best bits for barbecuing from our cow mates are the rump, fillet and sirloin, all of which are found along the top of the beast – the area that does the least work. From here you get t-bone steaks, sirloin steaks, rump steaks, fillet steaks and porterhouse steaks. The shoulders and lower legs – which do the most work – are cheaper cuts. They have loads of flavour but they require longer cooking times.

T-BONE

SIRLOIN/
PORTERHOUSE

RUMP

TOPSIDE &
SILVERSIDE

FILLET

LEG

SHEEP CUTS

Jokes about New Zealand and Sheep have helped us Aussies in endless arguments about sport ... sure we lost the game but at least we don't 'love' sheep. A get out of gaol free card we have needed many times after playing the formidable All Blacks in NZ.

For the sake of our sporting arguments NZ can keep the sheep, but lamb is ours.

Is it really a BBQ without lamb chops?

Also barbecuing 101 states that mastering your BBQ isn't complete until you look around your BBQ to see your mates with a beer in one hand and a juicy lamb rib straight from the BBQ in the other.

But our much loved lamb delights don't stop here. There's also the late night lamb kebab. These tend to appear on nights when it's too late, too dark and you're too far gone to BBQ your own lamb but

somehow when you wake up the next morning there always seems to be a discarded lamb kebab wrapper.

Our pacific neighbours might be nice and warm in their newly knitted woolen jumpers, but our barbecues keep us warm in winter as we BBQ beautiful lamb snacks.

SHOULDER

Like the cow, the meat that comes from the top of the sheep is the most tender. Cutlets are quick and fast and a rack of lamb looks pretty impressive. For kebabs go for cuts like neck and leg fillet. For a quick but spectacular barbecue offering get your butcher to butterfly a leg of lamb. It's happy to be left alone on the barbie while you have a beer, and there is no bone to worry about when carving.

CUTLETS &
RACK OF LAMB

LOIN CHOPS

CHUMP STEAK

LEG FILLET

LEG

SHANKS

BREAST

LEG STEAK

BANGERS FOR SANGERS

Along came the barbecue and the very next day came the sausage. What an ingenious idea, the creation of another way to eat meat.

We all know the quality of sausages varies greatly depending upon the ingredients used, and it's not hard to pick a bad snag. One of two things happen. Either the snag blasts open, midway through cooking or your BBQ catches fire from all the burnt fat.

Snags are by far the most versatile food at a BBQ. They'll cook just the same whether you line them up neatly or randomly throw them on the plate. You can eat them hot or cold, with or without sauce, plates or cutlery and they provide a brilliant fallback option to snack on at the start or end of the BBQ.

Gone are the days when we only had one variety of snag to choose from. Now there are a range of flavours available such as beef, chicken and pork all infused with an array of herbs and spices.

Good or bad, your hungry mates will still steal them from your plate.

HOTPLATE OR GRILL
TIME TO COOK: about 20 minutes

VEGGIES MATE!

At first glance some of these may seem like foreign objects, others may take you back to horrible childhood memories of things you were forced to eat after all your meat had been devoured and before you were allowed sweets.

After extensive research we have discovered interesting facts about these strange new BBQ products. Firstly, instead of walking around in paddocks or swimming in the ocean like the various other BBQ foods, these grow on trees and bushes and below the ground. They are also packed full of vitamins and minerals that help your body.

Most surprisingly, once you move past the fact that they're not meat, they actually taste great and add new flavours to the BBQ – when barbecued of course!

We challenge you to find a vegetable that doesn't taste great on a BBQ.

You can find veggies in the supermarket (look near the meat aisle) or at a green grocer (just like a butcher but for veggies) but we strongly recommend starting your own veggie patch at home. This way they will always be fresh, chemical free, you'll have more money for beer and you'll have another excuse to spend more time outdoors doing as little as possible. A veggie patch also acts as a great cover fieldsman in backyard cricket. ▷

THYME

SEA SALT

CAJUN

PIRI PIRI

TARRAGON

SAGE

FENNEL SEEDS

BARBEQUE SMOKEY
SEASONING

CHINESE FIVE SPICE

CORIANDER

ROSEMARY

PAPRIKA

CORIANDER

MINT

HERBS
AND SPICES

Buy fresh herbs either in pots or in bunches. If you buy
bunches keep them fresh by wrapping them in damp
kitchen paper, then store in a plastic bag in the salad
crisper of your fridge. You'll get the most flavour from the
herbs when they are either bruised or chopped, as this
releases the essential oils.

BASIL

FLAT LEAF PARSLEY

THYME

PARSLEY – We have used Flat-leaf (also called Italian) parsley in our recipes. Use it in marinades and sauces or use loads of the leaves in salads for added flavour.

MINT – Mint goes very well with potatoes so is delicious in potato salad. It's also ideal in Middle Eastern-style marinades and sauces or just add a handful to an Asian noodle salad.

BASIL – Where would a tomato salad be without basil? A delicious herb that just shouts summer. Chop some up and add to mayonnaise, add a little to French dressing or scatter a handful over sliced tomatoes with a drizzle of good olive oil and a dash of balsamic vinegar.

THYME – Thyme is a more woody herb, but its leaves are soft. It has quite a strong flavour but is great in marinades. For a speedy way to add flavour, dip a small bunch of thyme into seasoned olive oil and use as a basting brush for meat and fish while cooking.

CORIANDER – One of those herbs that you love or hate! For the lovers amongst us, chop up and add to marinades for fish, chicken or pork. Its intense aromatic flavour also goes very well with chilli.

DRIED HERBS AND SPICES – It's useful to keep a few jars of herbs and spices in your cupboard for adding instant flavour. When using dried herbs use in small quantities as they have an intense flavour. However, they don't really keep for more than 6 months before they start to lose their flavour, so buy in small quantities.

THYME – Dried thyme is one of the more useful dried herbs to keep in your cupboard. Use sparingly in marinades or in rubs. It's particularly good with chicken and fish.

SEA SALT – It's generally not a good idea to salt meat before you cook it on the barbie as this can draw out the delicious juices. Salt the meat after it is cooked. Sea and rock salt are delicious scattered over root vegetables when baking.

CAJUN – A mixture of spices ideal for flavouring fish, chicken, meat and prawns. Usually contains paprika, cayenne, garlic, oregano, thyme, salt and pepper. It is not necessarily fiery hot.

PIRI PIRI – This is a very spicy, small chilli pepper which can be bought ground, flaked or as a sauce. Good in spice rubs, marinades and bastes. A handy spice to keep in your cupboard.

TARRAGON – Unfortunately, this often bears little resemblance to fresh tarragon and loses its flavour quickly, so buy in small quantities. Use in rubs or sauces.

GROUND CORIANDER – With quite a different taste to the fresh leaves this is the ground up seeds of the coriander plant. Used widely in Middle Eastern-style cooking. Mix with some olive oil and rub over lamb chops before barbecing.

FENNEL SEEDS – These have an aniseed-liquorice flavour and taste slightly sweet. Good for rubbing onto the skin of oily fish before barbecuing or try rubbing some into pork chops or pork loin.

BARBECUE SMOKY SEASONING – This is a good mixture to buy if you don't want to have a wide variety of spices in your cupboard. Use either as a rub on its own or combine with olive oil and brush over meat or fish as it cooks to add both flavour and moisture.

CHINESE FIVE SPICE – This is an easy-to-find blend of spices, consisting of equal parts Sichuan pepper, cassis or cinnamon, fennel seeds, star anise and cloves. Particularly good with beef and pork.

DRIED CORIANDER – Dried coriander is the ground up seeds of the coriander plant. It's useful in marinades and fantastic when you want a North African or Asian flavour. Don't keep it too long otherwise it will just end up taking like musty dust!

DRIED ROSEMARY – This is a strongly flavoured herb, so use sparingly. Good with sausages and pork.

PAPRIKA – Paprika can range in flavour from mild to hot, so use sparingly if you're not sure how hot yours is, although it should say somewhere on the label. Combine with a little olive oil and brush over meat before and during barbecuing. Serve with a little lemon squeezed over.

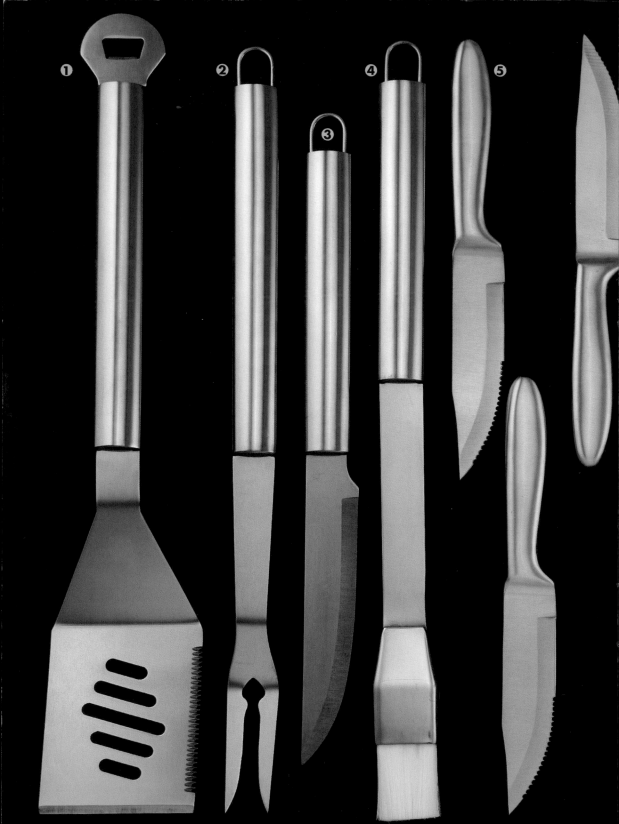

THE ESSENTIAL UTENSILS GUIDE

There's a shed-load of tools you could get for your BBQ. Here's a list for starters …

1 Oversized 3-in-1 tool
2 Fork
3 Cutting knife
4 Nylon basting brush
5 Steak knives
6 Corn holders
7 Skewers
8 Grill brush
9 Tongs

3 BEER RATING

WHOLE FISH BAKED WITH FENNEL AND TOMATOES

Make sure the fish has been very well scaled then rinse under cold running water. Pat dry inside and out. Make several shallow diagonal cuts across the fish then repeat in the other direction so you have a diamond pattern. Turn over and repeat on the other side.

Stuff the cavity with the slices of fennel, tomato and olives and 3 of the dill sprigs. Roughly chop the remaining dill and mix with 2 tablespoons of the oil and the juice of 1 lemon wedge. Season with salt and pepper.

Make a double layered piece of aluminium foil, large enough to completely enclose the fish. Brush the foil well with the remaining oil so the fish doesn't stick. Put the fish on the foil and spoon over the dill dressing, gently rubbing it into the cuts. Completely enclose the fish.

Preheat your barbecue flat plate to medium–low. Cook the fish for 10 minutes then carefully, using a fish slice or similar, turn the fish over and cook for a further 8–10 minutes. Carefully open the foil and check if the fish is cooked. It should flake easily at the thickest part; if not cook it for a minute or two longer.

Transfer the fish to a plate and serve with any cooking juices poured over and the remaining lemon wedges.

PREP: 20 minutes
COOK: about 20 minutes
SERVES: 4

1 whole snapper, about 2kg, gutted and scaled
1 small fennel, very thinly sliced
1 firm, ripe tomato, sliced
8 pitted black olives, thinly sliced (optional)
5 sprigs fresh dill, or flat-leaf parsley
3 tablespoons (¼ cup) olive oil
1 lemon, cut into 6 wedges
Salt and pepper

RISSOLES - WORLD'S BEST

1 BEER RATING

Mix all the ingredients (except the flour) together in a bowl until well combined – use your hands to do this.

Add half of the flour and bind – wet your hands then take about 3 tablespoons of mixture and roll into a round ball, then shape into a fat sausage shape. If the first rissole falls apart, add a little more flour to the mixture and mix.

Repeat with the remaining mixture.

Preheat your barbecue to hot. Oil the hot plate and cook the rissoles for about a couple of stubbies (8–0 minutes), turning occasionally.

These are great with salad or inside crusty bread rolls.

PREP: 15–20 minutes
COOK: 8–10 minutes
MAKES: 12–14

1kg good-quality lean beef mince
1 onion, chopped
Salt and pepper
1 egg, lightly beaten
2 tablespoons plain flour
Salad, barbequed red capsicum and crusty bread rolls, to serve

THE GARDEN SALAD RHYMING RECIPE

This is not a poem but rather a ballad,
Explaining how to best make the best garden salad,

It's become a tradition because of the heat,
That salad's the choice to accompany meat,

Follow this guide to gain extra flavour,
Earn brownie points to offset misbehaviour:

Fill a big bowl with iceberg lettuce,
You don't need much more, just don't get precious,

Now add some guacamole for a little more green,
It's the base of the best salad you've seen.

With cherry tomatoes and finely sliced capsicum,
Add cheese which is yellow and makes it taste yum,

Forget about making your own salad dressing,
The ones at the grocer come with my blessing,

French or Italian will add a flavour that's nice,
No need for sugar or any extra spice,

This will accompany any meat cooked on the day,
It's quick and easy-leaving more time to play,

Simple things often taste the best,
Make it the way you like it and it'll be loved by the rest.

TOP TIP #1
These are fabulous served with the tequila mayonnaise on page 36.

TOP TIP #2
For instant added flavour, squeeze some lemon juice over the rissoles just before serving.

TOP TIP #3
There's loads of other ingredients you can add, just make sure they are finely chopped. Try sun-dried tomatoes, olives, soft herbs such as parsley, chives or basil, or grated carrot.

ASIAN BARBECUED PORK LOIN

1 BEER RATING

Combine all the ingredients, except the pork, and whisk well to ensure the honey is dissolved. Put the pork in a shallow dish and pour the marinade over it. Turn the pork a couple of times to make sure it is well coated. Leave to marinate for at least an hour in the fridge and up to 24 hours.

Preheat barbecue flat plate to medium–high. Remove the pork from the marinade, allowing any excess to drip off, reserving the marinade to use again later. Cook the pork, turning 2 or 3 times and basting with the marinade regularly for 20–25 minutes or until cooked to your liking. Transfer to a plate by the side of the barbecue where it is warm and cover with foil. Leave to rest for 5 minutes. Serve cut in thick slices.

PREP: 10 minutes (plus 1-24 hours marinating, optional)
COOK: 20–25 minutes
SERVES: 8

2 teaspoons sesame oil, not vital but it sure does enhance the flavour
125ml (½ cup) runny honey
4 tablespoons (⅓ cup) soy sauce
2 tablespoons lemon juice
3 garlic cloves, crushed
5cm knob of fresh ginger, finely grated
1 teaspoon Chinese five spice (optional)
Black pepper
1.5kg pork fillet

TOP TIP

Any leftovers make a great Thai pork salad. Thinly slice the meat and combine with torn up lettuce leaves, halved cherry tomatoes, chunks of cucumber and plenty of fresh coriander and mint leaves. For the dressing combine 1 part fish sauce, 1 part light olive oil, 2 parts lime juice and a pinch of sugar – adjust these quantities until it tastes good. Add a finely chopped red chilli, a finely chopped kaffir lime leaf and some finely chopped lemon grass. Pour over the salad, toss and serve.

WHY BARBECUING IS BETTER THAN SEX!

- You don't have to clean your room before a potential BBQ.
- Gas at a BBQ is welcome.
- If your BBQ turns ugly there's no obligation to stay.
- Spraining your ankle at a BBQ is easy to explain to your boss.
- You will not lose mates if you invite their sisters to a BBQ.
- You can buy a marinade, not a serenade.

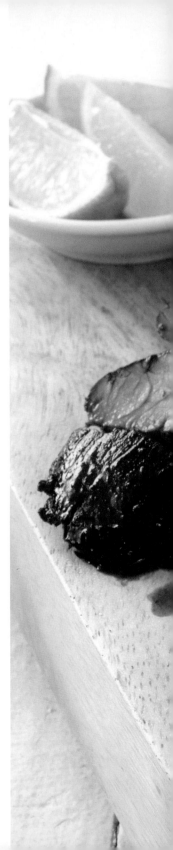

SPICE RUBS

Spice rubs can either be rubbed on in advance or just before you cook. If you've got cubes of meat or fish, a quick way to do this is to put the spice rub ingredients in a plastic bag, then add the cubes of meat or fish and shake the bag about to coat.

LEMON AND BLACK PEPPER – Great on steaks or chicken
Finely grate the zest of a lemon and mix with lots of freshly ground black pepper. Brush the meat with oil then rub over the mixture.

HOT AND SPICY – Ideal for fish and chicken
Combine 4 tablespoons finely chopped fresh flat-leaf parsley with 2 crushed garlic cloves, 2 teaspoons ground cumin, 2 teaspoons paprika and ¼ teaspoon ground chilli.

SPICE RUBS AND BASTES

If you haven't got much time, then spice rubs and bastes are great for adding instant flavour to pieces of meat and fish.

AROMATIC – Ideal for pork, lamb and beef
Combine 1 teaspoon ground cumin, 2 teaspoons ground coriander, 1 teaspoon ground cardamon and 1 teaspoon freshly ground black pepper.

SEEDY SPICE RUB – Great on steaks and chops
Crush 1 tablespoon coriander seeds (either with a pestle and mortar or put them in a plastic bag and bash them with whatever is to hand). Combine with 1 teaspoon cumin seeds, ½ teaspoon chilli flakes and a good grinding of black pepper. Brush the meat with a little oil, then rub on the spices.

BASTES

Bastes should be brushed on before you cook and then again a couple of times during cooking. It's best not to add salt to the mixture as this draws moisture out of the meat – salt the food after it is cooked.

CHINESE-STYLE BASTE – All these ingredients are available either in a good supermarket or an Asian supermarket
   Crush 4 garlic cloves and put in a bowl with 1 teaspoon black pepper, ½ teaspoon Chinese five spice powder, 1 tablespoon sesame oil, 1 tablespoon Chinese rice wine (or white vinegar), 1 teaspoon sugar and 2 tablespoons soy sauce.

ORANGE AND SOY BASTE – Ideal for meat and fish
   Combine 2 tablespoons of honey with the grated rind and juice of 1 orange, 2 tablespoons soy sauce, 2 crushed garlic cloves and 1 tablespoon grated fresh ginger.

HONEY MUSTARD BASTE – Great on sausages, pork, beef and chicken wCombine 2 tablespoons wholegrain mustard, 2 tablespoons honey, 1 tablespoon soy sauce, 2 tablespoons vegetable oil and plenty of ground black pepper.

THAI BASTE – This requires a bit of chopping and is great on fish, chicken or pork.
   Finely chop 1 red chilli and the bottom 10cm of a stalk of lemon grass. Mix in a bowl with 2 crushed garlic cloves, the juice of 1 lime, 1 tablespoon fish sauce, 1 teaspoon sugar, 1 tablespoon honey and 1 tablespoon vegetable oil.

BEER-CAN CHICKEN

2 BEER RATING

Beer-Can Chicken is relatively un-known in Australia, but it's an institution throughout the US. Beer-Can Chicken is achieved by indirectly roasting the chicken as you normally would, with the beer can as a roast holder.

We can all appreciate the versatility of cans – they hold beer, they don't break, they chill quickly and now they help roast chicken.

Beer-Can Chicken is a spectacular sight to see. To open the hood of your BBQ and to see a chicken standing up, mounted on a beer can is something you can't take seriously and don't forget in a hurry.

Besides its comical value, when you think about the concept it makes a lot of sense: usually, to keep meat moist while roasting you need to add a tin of water. Well beer works the same way, only with the added benefit of flavour.

The important thing to remember is to always open the can first (as a reminder, use some of the beer beforehand as a marinade) and use an aluminium 1 piece can, without welds or joints – as most Aussie cans are.

Once you have tried this and mastered the set-up and avoided the chicken falling over mid roast, you'll be hooked and never go back to standard chicken roasting again.

MUST BE COOKED UNDER
A HOODED OR KETTLE BARBECUE

PREP: 5 minutes
COOK: about 1 hour 10 minutes
SERVES: 4–5

1.8kg chicken
1 tablespoon oil
Black pepper
1 can of beer

HOW TO COOK THE CHOOK

Wash the chook inside and out and pat dry with paper towel. Rub the skin with some oil and season with black pepper. Open the beer can and do as you wish with half of it, perhaps even drink it, then carefully insert the beer can up the chicken's bottom.

Use an indirect heat to cook the chook – heat the two side burners to medium–hot. Put the chook on the middle of the flat plate, making sure it's well balanced and close the hood. Leave it to cook. Try not to let your mates open the hood too many times for a bit of a laugh as you will let too much heat out.

Carefully remove the can before carving.

TOPICS TO DEBATE AT A BBQ

- ☐ Who has more personality: your boss or your dog?
- ☐ Is it ok to spend your kids' Uni fund on a new BBQ?
- ☐ Who really wears the pants in your relationship?
- ☐ Why you are a better batsman than the current test openers.
- ☐ Who is the better Star Wars chick: Carrie Fisher or Natalie Portman?

REASONS WHY IT'S OK TO SPEND YOUR KIDS' COLLEGE FUND ON A NEW BBQ

Let me be the first to say your kids' education is very important. But let's be honest – unlike barbequing, an education isn't essential for the survival of the human race.

Below are 10 flawless excuses for blowing cash on a new BBQ. Feel free to use them on the occasions when you are required to explain why you need to spend the equivalent of your kids' college fund on a new BBQ.

1 SURVIVAL
Food is essential to life. A BBQ makes it possible to turn large beasts into food, preventing starvation. Without a BBQ we would all die from starvation.

2 EVOLUTION
It is important for humans to remain at the top of the food chain. Our BBQ reminds other animals that we still rule the kingdom.

3 ACADEMIC DEVELOPMENT
Heated debates while standing around the barbie stimulate the mind in the same way challenging questions and tests by teachers lead to the intellectual growth of their students. How else would we learn about the moon landing, important sporting achievements of our decade and every Seinfeld episode by name?

4 BECAUSE YOU CAN

5 SOCIAL DEVELOPMENT
A BBQ encourages interaction between members of the community. Without it, we run the risk of becoming inarticulate beer-swilling hermits.

6 PERSONAL WEALTH
An investment is defined as 'something that grows in value over time'. This refers not only to material items but one's personal happiness. Clearly relevant to barbecues, that result in endless weekends of enjoyment. The enjoyment and happiness provided is compounded with each use, in effect making a BBQ a growing asset.

7 FAMILY HAPPINESS
A BBQ allows the family unit to operate with less conflict. There will be fewer fights over who has to slave over the hot stove or clean the oven – especially during hot summer periods.

Guaranteed to get you some brownie points: suggest your lovely lady take a long bath while you slave over the hot BBQ – that is, lounge around with a beer while the BBQ does all the hard work.

8 HEALTH AND WELLBEING
Barbecuing ensures many harmful fats in foods are burnt off or drained away, reducing the chance of harmful conditions such as obesity.

The BBQ also promotes exercise by walking out into your backyard, followed by extensive exposure to fresh air, which is rich in oxygen – an essential element of wellbeing.

Plus because your family is happy (point 7) you will be less stressed and subsequently healthier.

9 WORLD PEACE
Umm, well it isn't really a reason, but who doesn't love the Miss Universe pageants. They all pick world peace as the answer, so who am I to argue?

IN CASE OF AN EMERGENCY
If points 1-9 fail to convince your audience that it's ok to spend your kids' Uni fund on a new BBQ, then it's essential to commit the following reply to memory. Remember, for this to be effective, you will need to practise it many times. These words may not come easily for some:

"There is nothing more important to me that my bar ... I mean ... my ... "

See, it's not so easy is it?

"There is nothing more important to me than my ... kids' education, that's right my kids' education."

BARBECUE ETIQUETTE

First things first: the BBQ owner is king and all those bringing alcoholic beverages to the event are royalty. Black isn't burnt, it's just well done and no-one is allowed to criticise the chef. The following tips will ensure you are the coolest guy at the BBQ.

REASONS FOR HAVING A BBQ

It could be sport, good weather, or no real reason at all. Australians don't need an excuse for a BBQ.

FASHIONABLY LATE

If you are the best friend you must be the first to arrive. You are responsible for helping to set up, ensuring all wanted friends are invited, and that adequate beer is at hand.

WHAT TO BRING

■ The host will provide the venue, the BBQ, nibbles and some cheap beers, wines and meat as emergency backups in case you run out.
■ BYO – for large BBQs you will generally bring your own meat and alcohol; sometimes salad will be supplied.
■ All catered – for smaller BBQs the host will generally supply all food and general drinks but it is proper etiquette to bring your own alcohol, that is, a slab.

WHO SHOULD YOU INVITE?

BBQs are not formal occasions where you should feel you need to invite certain people. They are in essence an informal gathering of friends to have a good time. If you don't like anyone or they are hard work, don't invite them, it's that simple.

WHAT TO WEAR

BBQs are never formal occasions. Shorts, beach shirts and thongs are all acceptable.

TIMING

Weekends and late afternoons, often extending into the evening. There are no hard and fast rules here, just whenever you feel like it.

IN- OR OUT-DOORS

Is there really any question: real men do it outdoors.

DESIGNATED DRIVER

Essential. Alternatively, catch a cab, leaving no temptation to drive and no temptation to only drink soft drink.

ENTERTAINMENT

Music or the soothing sounds of background cricket commentary. Remember the host is allowed to play whatever crap music he enjoys for at least an hour, then it's majority rule.

SINGLES

It is only manners to invite at least three single females for every single male.

BEST MATE ALLOWANCES

It's not wrong to kick your best mate out when he's semi-passed out on your lounge at 2am and it has been a few hours since everyone else has left, especially when you have to work the next morning. Alternatively, throw a blanket over him – either way you'll have a laugh in the morning.

On the flip side, your best mate has the right to pass out on your lounge and refuse to go home long after everyone else has left. It's just etiquette.

PREPARING FOR THE BIG DAY

PERHAPS THE MOST DIFFICULT PART of cooking a BBQ is the art of looking busy when you really aren't. Once you've mastered this, you will be guaranteed a day free of all household duties while remaining in the good books with your good lady.

The following are training techniques to ensure you are suitably prepared for the big day.

FLEXIBILITY

You must be flexible enough to change between different types of beer, from cans to bottles and, finally, onto spirits when the time is right.

You must also be flexible enough to adapt and overcome all situations without hesitation, for example, beer substitutes for marinade if you run out (not vice versa).

COORDINATION

It takes a tremendous amount of balance and coordination to carry three schooners and a pair of tongs 10 metres, avoiding eskies, deck chairs and various sporting equipment.

STAMINA

A nice mid afternoon BBQ can quickly turn into a 12 hour marathon. It is essential that you have enough stamina to last the distance. To increase your stamina try the following training techniques.
• Look into a mirror and tell as many tall tales as possible without laughing at your own dry humour.
• In practice for backyard cricket stand next to the clothes line for as long as you can practising one-hand one-bounce catches without spilling any beer.
• Get your BBQ nice and hot, stand down wind from the smoke and eat hot snags after they have been dropped onto the ground.

CONVICTION

It's important to remember exactly why you walked into the kitchen. If you forget, always come back with alcohol and argue that you didn't have enough hands so you had to prioritise and beer was the most obvious choice.

HYDRATION

Dehydration can lead to loss of concentration and possible injury. Similar to the way drink driving is dangerous, so is drink barbecuing. Remember to keep hydrated to avoid stupid injuries that quickly ruin a day of fun.

MOBILITY

To allow greater mobility when confronted with disastrous questions that could end the day's fun, I have pre-prepared the following answers:

QUESTION: Can I bring the mother-in-law?
ANSWER: Of course you can. To tell you the truth, Bob (pick your most degenerate friend) mentioned how much he would like to meet your mother-in-law and discuss body piercing.

QUESTION: Why can't we turn the sport down so that we can concentrate on a meaningful conversation?
ANSWER: Pardon, what? What did you say? I can't hear you, did you want me to turn up the cricket?

QUESTION: Can I help you with the BBQ?
ANSWER: No, it's ok. It's really hot out here in the sun next to the hot BBQ. It's hard work but I'm happy to do it.

ASPARAGUS, POTATO AND GOATS' CHEESE SALAD WITH SUN-DRIED TOMATOES

2 BEER RATING

Cook the potatoes in boiling, salted water for 15–20 minutes or until tender. Drain well, then cut into halves or quarters and put into a serving dish with the tomatoes. Combine the oil and vinegar with plenty of salt and pepper and the parsley. Drizzle half over the potatoes and toss gently. Set aside.

Snap off and discard the woody ends (i.e. not the narrow tip) from the asparagus then cut the the stalks into thirds. Brush with a little of the dressing. Cook on a hot barbecue plate for about 3 minutes until tender, turning once or twice. Arrange on top of the potato salad with the goats' cheese. Drizzle the remaining dressing over. Can be served warm or cold.

PREP: 10 minutes
COOK: 20–25 minutes
SERVES: 4

750g waxy potatoes, such as chat, pink fir apple or kipfler
60g (½ cup) semi sun-dried tomatoes, preferably ones from the deli counter (not in a jar), halved if large
125ml (½ cup) olive oil
2 tablespoons white wine vinegar
Salt and pepper
2 tablespoons chopped fresh flat-leaf parsley
1–2 bunches asparagus
60g goats' cheese, crumbled or chopped into small pieces

TOP TIP

You really do need to get the waxy sort of potato for this dish as they have a much better texture when cooked and don't just break up and go mushy. Chats are particularly easy to find and are often the small ones sold in a bag, sometimes labelled as salad potatoes.

WHY BARBECUING IS BETTER THAN SEX!

- ☐ BBQs don't have angry fathers with big guns.
- ☐ If the kids catch you they won't develop a life-long stutter.
- ☐ It's cool that your parents still have BBQs.
- ☐ Food cooking too quickly isn't a problem.

GRILLED VEGETABLE SALAD WITH HALOUMI AND DRESSING

2 BEER RATING

Slice the zucchini and eggplant into lengthways slices about 5–10mm thick. Cut the haloumi into 5mm thick slices crossways then chill until needed. Slice the capsicum into strips about 2cm wide and remove the seeds and membrane. Combine 4 tablespoons of the oil with the garlic and salt and pepper. Put the vegetables into a large bowl (you may need to do this in batches), add the garlic oil and toss to coat.

Preheat the barbecue to medium–high. Cook the vegetables on the grill plate for about 2 minutes on each side, checking them occasionally until they are soft and have good grill stripes on them.

Put all the vegetables on a serving platter. Combine the remaining oil with the capers and some salt and pepper and pour over the vegetables, tossing them gently to coat. Just before you are ready to serve, cook the haloumi on the flat plate for 30–60 seconds on each side – it melts pretty quickly so watch out. Arrange on top of the vegetables and scatter over the basil leaves.

PREP: 10 minutes
COOK: 15–20 minutes
SERVES: about 6, although you can easily serve more or less just by changing the amount of vegetables

2 zucchini
2 eggplants
250g block haloumi cheese
2 red capsicums
1 yellow capsicum
7 tablespoons (140 ml) olive oil
2 garlic cloves, crushed
Salt and pepper
2 tablespoons capers, chopped (optional)
1 tablespoon balsamic vinegar
Handful fresh basil leaves, shredded

TOP TIP #1
Don't cook the haloumi in advance as it goes rubbery when it cools.

TOP TIP #2
We know what you're thinking. How did a bunch of salads and veggies sneak their way into a real men BBQ book? Give these a go and you'll learn the answer for yourself. You've never really tasted veggies until they've been cooked on the BBQ.

This is the perfect side dish for any BBQ roast and it will impress the pants off your vegetarian friends who are used to receiving bread and bland plastic-like tofu at your barbecues.

VEGGIE FRITTATA

1 BEER RATING

PREP: 10 minutes
COOK: About 16 minutes
SERVES: 4–6

6 eggs, lightly beaten
Slosh of milk
85g (2/3 cup) grated cheese
Salt & pepper
1–2 tablespoons vegetable or olive oil
1 onion, chopped
About 170g (1½ cups) of cooked vegetables you have available – peas, corn, spuds, sweet potato, capsicum, roughly chopped – these can be leftovers or cooked fresh and chopped up quite small

Combine the eggs, milk, cheese and salt and pepper in a jug or bowl.

Preheat barbecue to medium–low. If your frying pan has a plastic handle wrap it in foil to protect it from the heat. Heat the oil in the pan on the barbie. Add the onion and vegetables and cook for about 5 minutes.

Pour in the egg mixture and tilt the pan around to ensure it is evenly spread, then cook for about 3 minutes. Cover with a lid or a piece of foil and cook for a further 8 or so minutes or until the top sets. The time it takes to cook will depend on the size of your pan and the temperature of your barbie. Don't have the barbie too hot otherwise the bottom will burn before the egg sets.

TOP TIP #1
This is ideal camping food for breakfast or dinner. It's filling and healthy too!

TOP TIP #2
A frying pan about 22-24cm in diameter is ideal for the above quantities, but it will work with most pans. However, if your pan is really wide, it will cook much more quickly and you'll end up with a very thin frittata!

POTATO BAKE

1 BEER RATING

MUST BE COOKED UNDER
A HOODED OR KETTLE BARBECUE

PREP: 10 minutes
COOK: 35–40 minutes
SERVES: 4

Oil, for brushing
2 onions, sliced
4 large potatoes (about 500g) peeled and thinly sliced (or left whole, see method)
300ml (small bottle) cream
Salt and pepper
60g (½ cup) grated cheese, such as cheddar or tasty

Heat a hooded barbecue to medium–hot. Brush a casserole dish (or foil tray if you don't like washing up) with the oil. Add the onions and potatoes in layers, drizzling with cream and seasoning with salt and pepper as you go. Add the remaining cream and sprinkle with cheese. Cook in the hooded barbecue for numerous stubbies – about 35–40 minutes – until golden brown and bubbling and until the potatoes are soft when pieced with a knife. If it browns too quickly, cover it with foil.

For a speedy bake, pre-cook the potatoes in boiling water or microwave until tender, then slice thinly and continue as above. It should only take about 20 minutes to cook.

BAKED BRIE
Take a whole small brie or camembert and remove the wrapping, reserving the wooden box if it has one. Rewrap the brie in a piece of foil. Place directly onto a hot barbecue plate and cook for 4–5 minutes on each side, or until it feels really soft when you press it. Unwrap and either serve from the foil or return to its box. Serve with crackers and crusty bread at the end of the meal. Delicious.

GARLIC AND HERB BREAD
To make a long loaf about 50cm long, you'll need to soften but not melt, about 125g butter. Beat in 3 crushed garlic cloves and 2 tablespoons chopped fresh parsley and plenty of salt and pepper. For a bit of bite you could also add some chopped red chilli. Cut slices through the bread stopping before you go all the way through, about 3cm apart. Spread the butter generously in between the slices then wrap well in foil. Place directly on a medium hot barbecue plate for 6–8 minutes, turning once.

RICE SALAD

PREP: 15–20 minutes
COOK: 30–40 minutes
SERVES: 6

400g (2 cups) long-grain rice
1 large red capsicum
75g cashew nuts (optional)
80g thinly sliced hot salami (optional)
2 corn cobs or 420g can corn kernels,
drained
4 tablespoons olive oil
Juice of 1½ lemons
Salt and pepper
3–4 tablespoons chopped fresh flat-leaf
parsley

Cook the rice according to the packet instructions. Drain well then rinse briefly under cold water, leave to drain over a sieve, loosening it up with a fork occasionally to separate the grains.

Now, back to the barbie ... cut the capsicum into wide strips and remove the seeds and membrane. Brush on both sides with a little oil and cook on a hot barbecue for about 10 minutes, turning occasionally until slightly blackened and softened. Rub off the charred skin, this should be quite easy to do.

Cook the cashew nuts on the hotplate, tossing them about a bit for 1–2 minutes. Cook the salami briefly until crisp. If using the corn cobs cook them for about 7 minutes on the barbie until slightly blackened, turning them regularly. Carefully slice off the kernels by holding the cob vertically and slicing downwards, this is really pretty simple. If using the can of corn, just add the kerbnels straight to the salad. Cut the salami into small pieces using scissors.

Dice the capsicum and add to the rice with the salami, corn and nuts. Whisk together the oil and lemon juice and pour over the rice. Add plenty of salt and pepper and the parsley and mix everything together well. Serve warm or cold.

POTATO SALAD

PREP: 10 minutes
COOK: 20–30 minutes
SERVES: 4–6

6 potatoes, scrubbed
2 eggs
4 spring onions, finely chopped
250g (1 cup) good-quality whole-egg
mayonnaise
1 teaspoon mild or hot English mustard
Salt and pepper

Put the spuds into a large pan of salted water. Bring to the boil, then cook for about 20 minutes or until just cooked – don't overcook them, but if you do, see the box below. Add the eggs to the boiling water and cook for 7 minutes. Cool in cold water then peel and chop.

Leave the potatoes to cool a bit, then peel (if necessary) and cube. Put in a bowl with the spring onions, mayonnaise, mustard and eggs and season with salt and pepper. Combine gently so as not to mash it too much. If you want it a bit more fancy add some or all of the extras below and combine gently.

TOP TIP #1

If you do overcook the spuds, turn them into an upmarket mashed potato by adding sliced spring onions, garlic, butter, milk, cream cheese and whatever you can find in the cupboard.

TOP TIP #2

The basic recipe for the potato salad is delicious on its own, but if you want to jazz it up a bit try adding one or more of the following: 2 tablespoons lightly toasted pine nuts, 1 red capsicum, chopped quite small, 3 thinly sliced celery stalks.

ROASTED TOMATO AND PASTA SALAD

1 BEER RATING

Preheat your BBQ to a medium heat. Take two long pieces of foil and arrange them in a cross shape resting in a bowl. Put all the tomatoes in the middle. Combine the garlic and 2 tablespoons of the oil and drizzle over the tomatoes. Add plenty of salt and pepper. Enclose in the foil. Cook on the BBQ plate for 20 minutes. Cook the bacon on the barbeque until crispy, then cut into bite-sized pieces.

Meanwhile, cook the pasta in boiling, salted water according to the packet instructions. Drain well. Transfer to a serving bowl and add the remaining 2 tablespoons of oil then toss well.

Once the tomatoes are cooked, add to the pasta with the bacon and toss gently. Scatter the avocado and basil leaves over the top. Can be served hot, warm or cold.

OTHER CLASSIC SALADS
GARDEN – throw together some crunchy lettuce leaves, like cos, some chunks of ripe tomato and pieces of cucumber. Toss in a dressing of 2 parts olive oil to 1 part red or white wine vinegar. Season well. Extras to add include: sliced red onion, chunks of cheddar or tasty cheese and sliced mushrooms.

GREEK – for this you will need some good-quality Greek feta cheese, black kalamata olives, ripe tomatoes, Lebanese cucumber, red onion (optional) and green capsicum. Cut the ingredients as required into chunks or slices. Dress with 2 parts olive oil to 1 part white wine vinegar with a pinch of dried oregano and some salt and pepper. Sit on a bed of lettuce.

ROCKET AND PARMESAN – for a more up-market salad, fill a bowl with rocket leaves and toss in a dressing of 3 parts olive oil to 1 part balsamic vinegar. Then use a potato peeler to make shavings of parmesan and scatter these over the top along with some sea salt flakes and plenty of freshly ground black pepper.

CAESAR – there are various options for this, but the very basics that you need are crispy cos lettuce leaves, bread croutons (which you can buy in the supermarket) and parmesan shavings. Drizzle over a good-quality Caesar salad dressing and you're away. Optional extras include crispy barbecued bacon, cooked chicken breast, cubed avocado and cherry tomatoes.

PREP: 10 minutes
COOK: about 25 minutes
SERVES: 6–8

250g punnet cherry tomatoes
2 firm, ripe tomatoes, cut into large chunks
3 garlic cloves, crushed
4 tablespoons olive oil
Salt and pepper
250g (about 5 long rashers) rindless bacon
500g pasta shapes, such as penne
2 avocados, cubed
Handful fresh basil leaves (optional)

TOP TIP #1
You can also cook the tomatoes with the oil and garlic in a baking dish (without the foil) in the oven at 180°C for 20–25 minutes, until softened.

TOP TIP #2
If making in advance, don't chop the avocado until just before serving or it will go brown.

CURE FOR THE COMMON ...
HANGOVER

THE CAUSE
The factors to look out for that contribute to the overall severity of a hangover are:
- Alcohol – type, quantity
- Food – if you don't eat beforehand you have no one but yourself to blame. Remember: food following three shots and eight beers – although it tastes sensational – is too late and will have no effect.
- Sleep – each hour without sleep is like an extra couple of drinks
- Body weight – it's all about relativity, or so some grey-headed guy once said.

PREVENTION
Is the only cure, but what fun is that?

THE CURE
Once the damage is done I recommend the following approaches to downgrade your hanger from a cracking 5 Star hitter to a manageable 2–3 Star feeling of discomfort:

NON-ALCOHOLIC LIQUID
You know it, it's kind'a like beer only with no alcohol. Keep it simple: water or sports drinks. For the more adventurous you could also try milk before having any alcohol, but this is generally a bit of an each way bet.

TOAST
This is my sure fire favourite. Cook up a couple of pieces of toast on the BBQ, of course (see examples below for guidance), with loads of butter and Vegemite. Follow this with loads of non-alcoholic liquid. The water will re-hydrate you while the Vegemite will give you the much needed Vitamin B.

BIG BREAKFAST
The traditional big breakfast on the Barbie cannot be over-looked.
A bacon and egg roll.
Sausage and egg muffin with hash brown in the middle.

LAUGHTER
Thinking back at yesterday's successful barbie will take your mind away from your health.

HAIR OF THE DOG
Often as a last resort you can get right back on the horse and have another barbie. I don't think it really matters how or where, simply whatever you can stomach.

If in doubt combine all of the above!!

TOP TIP
Away on a camping trip, renting a cottage with friends or if you just can't face washing up lots of pans at the weekend, the barbecue brekkie is the answer. Just about anything you cook in your frying pan can be done on your barbecue – eggs, bacon, mushrooms, snags, tomatoes. Just toss it on and marvel.

To add extra oomph, combine some olive oil with crushed garlic and chopped chilli and brush this onto mushrooms while they are cooking.

GRILLED PINEAPPLE WEDGES WITH CHEAT'S LIME ICE CREAM

PREP: 10 minutes
COOK: 2 minutes
SERVES: 6

1 BEER RATING

1 litre good quality vanilla ice cream
1 lime
1 pineapple, peeled
2–3 tablespoons honey

Put the ice cream in the fridge to soften, but not melt entirely. Finely grate the zest from the lime and squeeze 2 tablespoons of juice. Scoop out the softened ice cream into a bowl (keeping the tub) and stir in the lime zest and juice. Return to the tub and re-freeze.

Cut the pineapple into thick wedges, removing the core. Brush the pineapple with honey and cook on a clean, hot barbecue grill plate for about 1 minute on each side. Serve with scoops of the ice cream – it tastes just like a pine-lime splice!

TOP TIP
It's important to buy good quality ice cream (Connoisseur or Sarah Lee) as some cheaper ones contain a lot of air: when you soften the ice cream you will loose this air and a good amount of ice cream too!

MARSHMALLOW AND FRUIT KEBABS WITH CHOCOLATE SAUCE

PREP: 10 minutes
COOK: about 2 minutes
MAKES: as many or as few as you like, but this quantity of sauce is enough for 10–15 kebabs

1 BEER RATING

CHOCOLATE SAUCE
300ml (small bottle) cream
100g good quality dark or milk chocolate, roughly chopped

KEBABS (per kebab)
3 fruit pieces such as strawberries, peaches and nectarines
3 marshmallows
Wooden or metal skewers

To make the chocolate sauce, put the cream in a small saucepan over a low heat and heat until hot, but not boiling. Add the chocolate and stir until it has melted and the sauce is combined. Do not be tempted to rush the sauce otherwise the chocolate could burn. Remove from the heat and leave to cool and thicken for about 10 minutes, but do not refrigerate. If you're making the sauce in advance, lay a piece of plastic wrap directly on the top to prevent a skin forming.

If using wooden skewers, soak them in water for an hour, to prevent them burning on the barbecue. If using strawberries, cut any large ones in half and cut the peach or nectarines into chunks. Thread the marshmallows and fruit alternately onto the skewers. Cook on a medium barbecue grill plate for about 1 minute, turning regularly. Don't cook them for too long otherwise the marshmallows will melt and disintegrate.

Serve accompanied by the warm chocolate sauce.

APPLE PIE - MY NANNA'S RECIPE

2 BEER RATING

To make the pastry, put all the dry ingredients in a bowl and mix. Using your fingers, rub the butter in the flour until it kind of looks like breadcrumbs and there are no big bits of butter left. Stir in the egg and squish together until it forms pastry. If it won't come together add a tablespoon or two of cold water, a bit at a time until it comes together. Form into a ball and put in the fridge for at least 30 minutes. This is important, otherwise your pastry will be very hard and not roll out.

To make the filling, put the apples in a saucepan and cook over a very low heat for 5 minutes.

Mix the sugar and cornflour in about 1 tablespoon of water and add to the apples. Mix gently. Cool while rolling out the pastry.

Roll out half the pastry on a floured work surface (or see tip below) then use to line a tin of about 18cm square. Add the apple mixture and moisten the edge of the pastry. Roll out the remaining pastry to cover the top of the pie then press the edges together with a fork to seal them. Make a couple of slits in the top to allow steam to escape. Chill until you cook it.

You need indirect heat to cook the pie. So heat the side burners on your barbecue to medium–low. If using a coal-barbie, heat the coals for about 45 minutes then put a baking tray on top of the coals, but under the grill rack. Reduce the heat to low and cook the pie under a hood for 40–50 minutes, or until the pastry is golden. Serve with custard, ice cream or cream.

MUST BE COOKED ON A HOODED OR KETTLE BARBEQUE

PREP: 40 minutes (plus 30 minutes to chill)
COOK: 40–50 minutes
SERVES: 4–6

PASTRY
125g (1 cup) plain flour
125g (1 cup) self-raising flour
1 tablespoon custard powder
2 tablespoons sugar
125g butter or hard margarine, cubed
1 egg, beaten

FILLING:
6 large Granny Smith apples, peeled, cored and sliced
2 tablespoons sugar
1 heaped tablespoon cornflour
Custard, ice cream or cream, to serve

TOP TIP
If you're no good at rolling out pastry, place a sheet of greaseproof paper/baking paper on the work surface and roll out the pastry on this. Then all you have to do is lift up the sheet of pastry, invert the pastry over the tin then peel off the paper.

SPECIAL THANK YOU
A special thank you goes to nanna for this BBQ gem. We all have fond childhood memories of filling up on freshly baked treats and everyone knows you can never make anything that's as good as your nanna's cooking. But on the BBQ this comes close.

Even the hard-core barbecuer may be surprised to see an apple pie cooked on the BBQ. There is no better way to finish a BBQ than with apple pie straight from the BBQ.

A VERY MOIST CHOCOLATE PUDDING

2 BEER RATING

You'll need a 1–1½ litre ovenproof dish for this. A shallower, rather than deep dish, is better, otherwise it won't bake properly. Grease the dish with a bit of butter.

Put the flour and 2 tablespoons of the cocoa into a bowl and whisk together to combine. Stir in 125g (½ cup) of the sugar and the grated chocolate. Combine the milk, egg and melted butter. Make a well in the centre of the flour mixture and pour in the milk mixture. Stir gently to combine, but do not overbeat. Pour the mixture into the dish.

Bring 200ml of water to the boil. Add the remaining cocoa and sugar and stir until dissolved. Pouring over the back of a spoon to help get an even layer, pour carefully and evenly over the chocolate mixture.

To cook. Heat the side burners on your barbecue to medium-low. Once hot, place the pudding in the centre, away from the indirect heat, and bake for about 30–40 minutes.

To check if it's is ready insert a skewer into the centre and leave it there for a couple of seconds, pull it out and if the stuff that is sticking to it is of a cake-like consistency, rather than wet, it is ready. If not cook it for a further 5–10 minutes or until cooked. If there is melted chocolate on the skewer this is OK. Serve with ice cream or loads of cream.

MUST BE COOKED IN A HOODED OR KETTLE BARBECUE

PREP: 20 minutes
COOK: 30–40 minutes
SERVES: 6–8

125g (1 cup) self-raising flour
40g (½ cup) cocoa powder
310g (1¼ cups) caster sugar
100g good–quality dark chocolate, grated
125ml (½ cup) milk
1 egg, lightly beaten
60g butter, melted
Icing sugar, to serve (optional)
Ice cream or thickened cream, to serve

READY, SET, GO ...

To get ready in advance, you can make this pudding up to the stage where you've poured the batter mixture into the dish up to an hour before you bake it. Pour the chocolate sauce over the top just before putting it in the oven. It will then be ready to eat once you've finished, but can also sit around for a bit – just don't forget it's in the oven. The longer you leave it to sit after baking the less sauce you will have because it will be absorbed back into the sponge.

TOP TIP #1
The cheat's lime ice cream from p108 is also delicious served with this.

TOP TIP #2
If you want to get a bit flash, sift some icing sugar over the top before serving.

TOP TIP #3
For extra kick add a little chopped red chilli to the milk and egg mixture.

TOP TIP #4
This is delicious eaten with a glass of dark porter beer.

TRIFLE

1 BEER RATING

Set both the jellies according to the packet instructions.

Chop up the jam roll and put in the bottom of your serving dish (you'll need a dish with about a 3 litre capacity). Pour the port or sherry evenly over the cake, then pour over the custard in an even layer. Chop up the jelly using a spoon and knife and spoon over the custard. Top with whipped cream and sprinkle the grated chocolate over the top. Chill until serving.

PREP: 20 minutes
COOK: no cooking
SERVES: 10–12

2 packets of jelly – your choice of colour – although if your barbecue is around an Australian sporting event, then you have no choice but to use yellow and green jelly
400g jam roll (no cream)
4 tablespoons (1/3 cup) port or sherry
2 x 500ml cartons extra creamy or premium vanilla custard, preferably Paul's brand
600ml thickened cream, lightly whipped
3 tablespoons (about 20g) grated dark chocolate, to serve

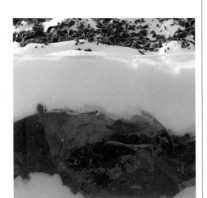

TOP TIP #1
You need to use a thick custard for this, otherwise the cream and chocolate will just sink into the custard.

TOP TIP #2
This is ideal for breakfast when you've got a hangover!

BUSH BBQ'S

SOMETIMES WE FORGET THE outdoors extends well beyond our own backyards. In Australia we are truly blessed with numerous parks, camping grounds and bush escapes where real men can do what they do best: BBQ outdoors, in the wild.

Just because you're in the middle of the bush, doesn't mean you can't enjoy a great BBQ feed. There are many options these days from the make-your-own traditional bush BBQ camp fire through to small kettle charcoal BBQs, Hibachis and other portable gas camping stoves.

It may be a little more challenging, but anything you cook at home on your flat-top BBQ it is possible to cook in the bush. The added benefit is the back-to-nature survivor satisfaction you receive from creating fire and living on what nature provides. Well, at least, creating fire with matches, fire-lighters and cooking a banquet from the esky, accompanied by icy cold beer.

FOR THE FIRST TIME BUSH BARBECUER YOU'RE IN FOR A TREAT IF YOU REMEMBER TO TAKE THE RIGHT EQUIPMENT

■ Take matches, firelighters, torch, spare batteries, esky, drinking water, a pan, a small camping BBQ, a billy, charcoal, insect repellant, basic cooking and eating utensils and icy cold beer.
■ If setting up camp, remember to pick level ground and clear major rocks before setting up your tent to ensure a nice comfortable sleep.
■ Get there early, not only to get the best spot but also to ensure you're not stuck setting up camp and your bush BBQ in the dark.
■ Block ice in your esky will last longer, ensuring your food stays fresh and your beer remains ice cold.

■ Keep your bush BBQ well away from your tent and overhanging trees and scrub that may catch fire, and clearly mark your, well … personal rest areas.
■ At the end of the last day's BBQ when all your ice has melted and you're ready to head home use the water from the esky to put out your bush BBQ.

WHY BARBECUING IS BETTER THAN SEX!

□ You are only expected to remember one position for your BBQ in the backyard.
□ Bumping into stinging nettles at a bush BBQ doesn't ruin your entire camping experience.

BEST BEERS F

CASCADE
Another reason why we love Tassie

TOOHEYS NEW
The beer of NSW known simply as 'New'

BLUE TONGUE
We love boutique beers and this is no exception

TOOHEYS EXTRA DRY
The perfect crisp, dry finish for hot summer barbies

OR THE DAY!!!

HAHN PREMIUM
A big name in beer and
an award winning lager

BEEZ NEEZ
Matilda Bay's unique
honey flavoured beer

COOPERS
Clear days and cloudy
beer, what a match!

VICTORIA BITTER
Proudly Victorian, with
great theme music

BACKYARD CRICKET – THE RULES

Pitch length – back door to back fence
Stumps – case of beer and a bin (you don't want to damage the case so put it at bowling end)
Hit cat – cheers from the crowd
Dog gets the ball – no runs allowed; chase (without spilling beer)
Ladies' involvement – of course, with much support and cheering
One-hand – one-bounce – out
Bat – beaten-up old bat essential
Ball – must be a tennis ball, never be tempted to use the real thing
Kids – help at any opportunity … carry them down the pitch
Broken windows (downside) – out
Broken windows (upside) – back to the BBQ and sit down with a beer
Neighbours' garden – 4 runs, but out
Two houses down – 6 runs, but out, I'm afraid (impressive result though)
Lost ball – out, everyone back to the BBQ

RECIPE INDEX BY BEER RATING

1 Beer – quick and easy
Quick and easy on a plate! 22-25
Prawns with tequila mayonnaise 26
Sticky pork ribs 28
Pork kebabs with herby mayo 32
Chilli and coconut marinated prawns 34
Steak sandwiches with simple balsamic onions 54
Lamb cutlets marinated in yoghurt and chutney 56
Crispy salmon steaks 62
Rissoles – world's best 82
Asian barbecued pork loin 84
Veggie frittata 100
Potato bake 100
Salad, Potato 102
Salad, roasted tomato and pasta 104
Salad, Caesar – ingredients only 104
Salad, Garden – ingredients only 104
Salad, Greek – ingredients only 104
Salad, Rocket and parmesan – ingredients only 104
Grilled pineapple wedges with cheat's lime ice cream 108
Marshmallow and fruit kebabs with chocolate sauce 108
Trifle 114
Spice rubs and bastes 86
Baked brie 100

2 Beer – a little more time required
Roast beef 46
Butterflied leg of lamb 42
Barbecued king prawns – sweet chilli or garlic 30
Portuguese chilli chicken burger 36
Barbecue pizza 38
Jumbo beef burgers 50
Chicken tikka kebabs with cucumber dip 52
Whole barbecued fish 60
Beer-can chicken 88
Asparagus, potato, goats' cheese salad with sun-dried tomato 96
Grilled vegetable salad with haloumi and dressing 98
Salad, Rice 102
Apple pie 110
Chocolate pudding 112

3 Beer – dress to impress meals
Roast chicken 40
Roast pork and veggies 44
Baby octopus salad 58
Whole fish baked with fennel, tomatoes, olives and herbs 80

INDEX BY RECIPE

GREEN – 1 BEER
ORANGE – 2 BEERS
RED – 3 BEERS

Apple pie   110
Asian barbecued pork loin   84
Asparagus, potato, goats' cheese salad with sun-dried tomato   96
Baby octopus salad   58
Baked brie   100
Barbecue pizza   38
Barbecued king prawns – sweet chilli or garlic   30
Beer-can chicken   88
Butterflied leg of lamb   42
Chicken tikka kebabs with cucumber dip   52
Chilli and coconut marinated prawns   34
Chocolate pudding   112
Crispy salmon steaks   62
Grilled pineapple wedges with cheats lime ice cream   108
Grilled vegetable salad with haloumi and dressing   98
Jumbo beef burgers   50
Lamb cutlets marinated in yoghurt and chutney   56
Marshmallow and fruit kebabs with chocolate sauce   108
Pork kebabs with herby mayo   32
Portuguese chilli chicken burger   36
Potato bake   100
Prawns with tequila mayonnaise   26
Quick and easy on a plate!   22-25
Rissoles – world's best   82
Roast beef   46
Roast chicken   40
Roast pork and veggies   44
Salad, Caesar – ingredients only   104
Salad, Garden – ingredients only   104
Salad, Greek – ingredients only   104
Salad, Potato   102
Salad, Roasted tomato and pasta   104
Salad, Rocket and parmesan – ingredients only   104
Spice rubs and bastes   86
Steak sandwiches with simple balsamic onions   54
Sticky pork ribs   28
Trifle   114
Veggie frittata   100
Whole barbecued fish   60
Whole fish baked with fennel, tomatoes, olives and herbs   80

Longueville Media
PO Box 102 Double Bay
New South Wales 1360 Australia
www.longmedia.com.au
info@longmedia.com.au
T. 02 9362 8441

Interior design by Justin Golby
Cover design Holy Cow! Design & Advertising
Food photography by Jon Bader, Contacts
Other Photography by Josh Evans and Ben Rollison, Studiogo
Food writing and styling by Katy Holder
Thank you to Barbeques Galore for providing a selection of BBQs

Cataloguing in Publication
Barnes, Joshua, 1978- .
Real men do it outdoors : the blokes'
BBQ cookbook.

ISBN 1 920681 20 5 (pbk).
1. Cookery, Australian. 2. Barbecue cookery - Australia. I. Title.

641.5784